Negative Images: A Simple Matter of Black and White?

An examination of 'race' and the juvenile justice system

BRUCE M. KIRK

Avebury

Aldershot • Brookfield USA • Singapore • Sydney

Published by
Avebury
Ashgate Publishing Limited
Gower House
Croft Road
Aldershot
Hants GU11 3HR
England

Ashgate Publishing Company
Old Post Road
Brookfield
Vermont 05036
USA

British Library Cataloguing in Publication Data
Kirk, Bruce
  Negative images : a simple matter of black and white : an
  examination of 'race' and the juvenile justice system
  1.Sentences (Criminal procedure) - England 2.Discrimination
  in criminal justice administration - England 3.Juvenile
  corrections - England
  I.Title
  364.3'6'0942

Library of Congress Catalog Card Number: 96-84834

Printed and bound by Athenaeum Press, Ltd.,
Gateshead, Tyne & Wear.

Contents

PART TWO

NEGATIVE IMAGES

APPENDICES

Figures and tables

Acknowledgements

Inevitably a piece of work of this order is not completed without considerable support from a variety of people and this is no exception. I would like to begin the process of acknowledging support by registering my thanks to Wolverhampton Social Services Department who commissioned the research upon which this book is based. In particular, I am indebted to colleagues in the Adolescent Services Team for their support and patience throughout the period of the study, especially, Thakor Patel, Hugh Thornbery and Alan Woodhouse. Also, I am grateful to Sylvia Horton who typed the questionnaires and to Roger Beach for his 'nearly' proof-reading skills!

Paul Cavadino paid me the highest honour by validating my research and its outcomes with his agreement to write the foreword. Richard Hester at the Rainer Foundation provided invaluable help in the most tangible form, namely through access to computer facilities at Rainer's Birmingham office. Magistrates and Justices' Clerks in three petty sessional divisions gave of their valuable time to organise the completion and return of data sheets that are central to the qualitative analysis of the study. Vanessa Bishop read 123 court reports and extracted terminology for analysis and Helen Gorman gave freely of her advice.

John Harris, my long time friend and mentor, stimulated the original proposal, maintained belief in the project and saw me through the blood sweat and tears. He read numerous drafts, advised and guided me and deserves considerable credit for this, the final product. Hilary Graham too, gave freely of her depth of knowledge in research methodology and design. Roger Evans' constructive criticism stimulated a number of developments in the script and Angela Munro picked up the study when it was in danger of gathering dust on the shelf and gave new momentum to the project of bringing it to a wider audience. Kathryn Craggs gave endless support and encouragement to the process and has been central to the process of moving on my thinking and awareness.

Most of all, I want to thank my family - Chris, Stuart and Laura - who, in so many ways 'paid' for the research through freely and unselfishly giving up the time they might reasonably have expected me to be with them. It is no coincidence to me that Laura's first words - 'bye-bye Dada' - were spoken during this time. Work on this project has, for her, lasted a lifetime and it was no fun for her or Stuart to have a largely absent father. Chris, in true partnership, shared my joy but more crucially supported me through my doubts and frustrations.

Finally, to my parents, thanks for nothing in particular and everything in general.

Wolverhampton
April 1996

Foreword

This stimulating and disturbing study helps to illustrate some of the reasons for the differential sentencing of Black defendants, and to increase our understanding of what can be done to combat racial injustice in the treatment of young offenders.

Based on an analysis of cases dealt with by the Wolverhampton juvenile court in 1990, Bruce Kirk shows that African-caribbean defendants received significantly more high tariff sentences (particularly supervision orders with requirements and community service orders) than white or Asian defendants - a distinction which could not be explained by differences in the seriousness of offences, and which occurred although African-caribbean defendants had on average committed fewer current offences and had shorter previous criminal records.

By analysing social inquiry reports, the study shows that reports were more likely to recommend high tariff sentences on African-caribbean defendants in circumstances where such recommendations would not have been made if the defendant had been white. While in general reports described African-caribbean defendants in a positive or balanced manner, report writers for well-intentioned reasons also included background information on defendants which was in practice likely to reinforce stereotypical views of Black families, thereby leading to more substantial intervention in the form of a high tariff sentence.

The author's proposals - including recommendations designed to boost the confidence of courts and the public in supervision orders, to remove stereotypical material from reports, to increase commitment to the principles and procedures of 'gatekeeping', and to concentrate pre-sentence report writing in specialist youth justice teams - deserve attention by everyone concerned to eradicate discriminatory practice from the youth justice system.

I am happy to commend this thoughtful and challenging study to members of all agencies involved in the youth justice process.

Paul Cavadino
Chair
Penal Affairs Consortium

Part One
The Backdrop

1 Introduction

In 1986, Wolverhampton Social Services Department undertook the first monitoring exercise examining sentencing outcomes of all cases heard in the local juvenile court (WMBC, 1987). Two findings that emerged from that exercise caused alarm amongst juvenile justice practitioners. First, it was noted that although African-caribbeans comprised a little under one-tenth of the 16 year old population in Wolverhampton they represented nearly one-quarter of all those who appeared in the juvenile court during the year. Even more startling was the finding that nearly a third of those African-caribbean defendants received custodial sentences.

Faced with this information it might have been easy to have drawn the simple conclusion that this was evidence of differential sentencing policy imposed within a racist juvenile justice system. An alternative explanation may have been that these outcomes reflected increased criminal activity on the part of African-caribbean young people in Wolverhampton. There were those who were not only clear why these outcomes had occurred but were clear too where the responsibility lay for it. However, the monitoring exercise itself was inconclusive. If the implications of the findings were going to be better understood it would be necessary to engage in a research project of greater depth.

Alongside the unresolved issues from the monitoring exercise there began to emerge concerns about the quality of Social Inquiry Reports (SIRs). Although there was a 'gate-keeping' panel in operation many reports were presented to the court without first being referred to the panel. Anecdotal evidence suggested that there were some examples of poor professional practice. Might it be that there was a link between differential sentencing outcomes and SIR practice?

A decision was made to conduct a study of all cases heard in the juvenile court in 1990. The purpose of the study was to consider the impact of the local justice system on offenders. It sought to bring about a deeper understanding of the sentencing process, set against the backdrop of the development of the juvenile justice system in England and Wales as a whole. As part of this process all cases heard in the court during the year would be analysed with particular emphasis on the possible influence of SIRs.

Court hearings are, of course, only a part of the whole justice process. The route taken from the point of arrest to the imposition of a sentence in a court hearing includes many key stages at which decisions are made which determine how to proceed. Wherever decisions are made there is scope for differential or prejudicial treatment and in order to determine the extent to which Black young people are disadvantaged within the justice system as a whole, systematic analysis would be required to examine each of the key, decision-making stages. Such a task was beyond the remit and scope of the study. The intention of this study was to focus on sentencing outcomes as one of a number of studies that were planned by agencies engaged in the local justice system.

Nevertheless, it is recognised that sentencing cannot be seen in isolation from the whole justice process. In order to examine sentencing patterns it is necessary to be aware of and understand the impact of other stages. Whilst, then, this study has concentrated on sentencing it does so in the context of the justice process as a whole. For example, it is apparent that whilst sentences are imposed by Magistrates their decisions are influenced by information and opinion offered by other actors in the system: crown prosecution service, defence solicitors, social workers, probation officers, etc. In such circumstances the eurocentric values of the dominant white culture would be communicated and may contribute to discriminatory sentencing processes. A second function of this study then, was to attempt to identify ways in which social work practice may be contributing to differential sentencing patterns.

The findings of the study are presented in two parts. In Part One Wolverhampton Juvenile Court is placed in the broader context of the juvenile justice system as it has developed in England and Wales and as it operates against a backdrop of pervasive racism. In order to locate the study of sentencing in a wider context it is necessary to situate the justice system within a racist society permeated by institutional racism. In chapter 2 I shall argue that although classical notions of 'race' have long since been discredited by the academic community, assertions of the existence of a

4

unique and superior white British 'race' are maintained in contemporary society just as they were used historically to justify British imperialism. The days of empire are gone but notions of the distinctiveness of the white British 'race' are perpetuated within the infrastructure, fabric and institutions of contemporary Britain. Institutions in Britain discriminate against people on the grounds of 'race', either directly, regardless of race relations legislation, or indirectly as institutional racism. They prevent the legitimisation of the experiences of Black people and hold back appropriate responses.

Although there have been attempts to outlaw discrimination, those attempts have been selective in their area of jurisdiction, unconvincing in application and lacking the necessary resources to be effective (Gordon, 1990). Whilst a view prevails that a 'colour-blind' approach ensures equality of service or treatment, racial minority people are consistently disadvantaged by institutions operating mono-cultural policies. This approach to equality is equivalent to that which advertises services to people with sight impairment through the medium of posters. Whilst the argument that sighted and sight impaired people are subject to the same advertising process, sight impaired people are clearly disadvantaged.

The justice system, as one of the cornerstone institutions of British society, is deemed to administer justice equally, without fear or favour. However, close inspection of agencies and practices inherent in the justice system consistently reveals over-representation of Black people at key stages within the system. I shall show that whilst the evidence of research may not be conclusive, the evidence of Black experiences is compelling.

The professions too, based as they are upon the norms and values of the dominant white culture, purvey racism, even though they purport to be committed to anti-racism, adopt equal opportunities policies and promote anti-discriminatory practices. In chapter 3 I shall demonstrate how the absence of a consideration of 'race' within the ideological stances that frames and inform the operation of the justice system consequently denies Black experience and perpetuates discrimination. An examination of social work practice as manifest in court reports follows in chapter 4 and reveals how Black people are portrayed stereotypically in language that is value-laden and which sustains prejudicial decision-making processes.

Social workers attempting to work to principles of anti-discriminatory practice are often faced with a dilemma when seeking to implement an anti-racist strategy. Either they articulate the issues and attempt to place them in a cultural context or else they avoid them. In both cases they run the risk of perpetuating the differential treatment of Black people. In circumstances

5

where anti-discriminatory principles are applied there are often unintended consequences that lead to Black people being disadvantaged. Consider, for example, the stigmatising and labelling experiences of lone parent families. Often held to exemplify all that is ill in family life and child rearing, lone parent families are simultaneously to be blamed and pitied. If those lone parent families are also Black then the prejudice is compounded and they become embodiments of an assault on the traditional British way of life. Clearly the experiences of prejudice which children and young people are confronted by daily impact upon behaviour and self esteem. However, to highlight the fact of their experiences of prejudice serves also to reinforce the prejudice itself. Therefore, a court report author may wish to refer to the experiences of a Black lone parent family in mitigation of offending behaviour. However, the message may not be received as one of mitigation but as an aggravating factor causing the defendant to be regarded as in need of a more punitive sentence in order to bring about deterrence the likes of which Black lone parent families may be unwilling or unable to achieve.

Discussion around 'race' and Social Inquiry Report practice is developed in chapter 5 to include considerations in relation to the juvenile justice system more widely. Attention is given to the alternative hypotheses that have been developed to explain the over-representation of African-caribbean people in the juvenile justice system, namely; that it is a consequence of institutional racism inherent in the key stages of the system or that it reflects higher levels of Black criminal activity. I shall draw on key features of the debate as manifest in literature, research and accounts of Black experiences of the justice system to argue that the over-representation of African-caribbean young people in the system cannot be explained by higher criminal activity.

Having considered in Part One, the juvenile justice system in overview, I go on, in Part Two, to present the study that was conducted in Wolverhampton. The structure and organisation of the social services department are described in chapter 6 and placed in the context of the local juvenile justice system as it operated in 1990.

The study comprises two components: a quantitative analysis of all 282 cases heard in Wolverhampton Juvenile Court in 1990 and a qualitative analysis of a sample of 123 social inquiry reports presented to the court during the year. The methodology utilised in each area of analysis is described in chapter 7.

The quantitative analysis was based on data routinely collected by Court Officers. From an initial profile of the cases the study moves on to analyse the characteristics of those cases where high tariff sentences were imposed, since it was in this area of sentencing outcomes that African-caribbeans were significantly over-represented. Data relating to high tariff disposals were analysed by 'race' in order to establish whether there were material differences between cases which might explain the over-representation. Thus the cases were analysed for differences in relation to the number and seriousness of the offences, the number of offences to be taken into consideration (tics), remand type and SIR recommendations.

The findings, which are presented in chapter 8, suggest that high tariff disposals were disproportionately imposed on African-caribbeans with fewer charges of similar seriousness and less antecedents or tics. It is apparent from the findings that this over-representation cannot be explained by the material facts of the cases, neither is it indicated by the remand type or SIR recommendation.

The qualitative analysis focused upon the content of social inquiry reports (SIRs), particularly insofar as they portrayed the individual offenders and their social background. Lengthy consideration was given to the methodology employed in other SIR content studies but few seemed to incorporate the "sentencer's eye view" and most were essentially impressionistic considerations of the report content. For the purposes of this study, which was attempting to tease out how report content was perceived by sentencers - Magistrates - and which needed to be measurable in order to make comparisons between reports written in relation to offenders of different racial origins, there appeared to be no readily available methodology which would serve the purpose of this study. It was necessary, therefore, to tailor-make suitable apparatus for the job in hand.

A two stage analysis was undertaken reflecting how individual characteristics were portrayed and how individuals were placed into the context of their social background. The first stage required the extraction of descriptive terms and phrases contained in SIRs. This material was then presented in documentary form to three groups of Magistrates drawn from benches outside Wolverhampton. Each Magistrate gave a score for each of the terms signifying whether a positive or negative impression of the offender was conveyed. By aggregating the scores it was then possible to award a score to each SIR which indicated the overall effect of the collective descriptive terms that were used. The findings are presented in chapter 9 together with the results of the second stage of the content analysis. This second stage focused upon causes of offending identified by SIR authors from the social background of the offenders concerned. When reports were analysed by 'race' it was noted that although African-caribbean defendants were generally portrayed more positively from whites as individuals, the causes of offending , as perceived by social workers, were presented in such a way that allowed stereotypical and prejudicial judgements to be made. Thus although individual African-caribbean defendants were portrayed relatively positively, they were set against a back drop of social background information which could be interpreted prejudicially and hence undermine the positive elements in the report.

From these findings conclusions and recommendations are made in relation to strategies for social work practice and changes in the organisational structure of the Social Services Department in an attempt to address the issues. These conclusions and recommendations are set out in chapter 10.

Upon conclusion of the study an initial report was produced and presented to the Departmental Management Group. Following consideration of the report organisational changes were made which brought SIR preparation largely under the umbrella of the Juvenile Justice Team as a means of: emphasising the distinctive nature of SIRs in contrast to most other reports that social workers routinely prepare: bringing SIR production under close control within a team whose workload focuses specifically upon young offenders and the juvenile justice system and encouraging greater consistency through the increased awareness of issues and trends in a team that had regular contact with the juvenile court.

Following closely on the heels of the publication of the first report but unrelated to it, came a number of developments. Most significant of these was the implementation of the Criminal Justice Act 1991 which introduced Youth Courts and replaced SIRs with pre-sentence reports (PSRs). These provisions, together with s.95 which outlawed discriminatory practices in the justice system and the establishment of national standards governing PSR production and community sentences appeared to put into place safeguards which would address some of the issues and concerns which arose out of the study. Most crucially, the notion of 'proportionality' introduced by the 1991 Act and of sentencing on the basis of seriousness of the current offence plus one other seemed to diminish the scope for differential sentencing.

In such circumstances the impetus for the research had become forgotten and the findings and recommendations had arguably been overtaken by events such that for many months the report sat gathering dust on the shelves. However, it has emerged that an insufficient beachhead had been established and some areas of progress have fallen back. In other ways expected changes in practice have not materialised rendering the messages of this research study more significant than was at one stage evident.

As a result, I have revisited the study; looked again at the glimpses and insights into court report practice and the implications for sentencing and thought again about the issues that emerge and remain of concern in the current youth justice system. I present this study, then, as an attempt to identify whether Black young offenders who appeared in court in 1990 were disadvantaged in court proceedings, consequently leading to more intrusive sentencing than if they had been white. The study is an attempt to determine whether there was scope for collusion, however unwitting, by social workers in discriminatory practices and seeks to make positive recommendations about the way in which youth justice practitioners and agencies might operate in an effort to counter discrimination.

I am concious of the onerous responsibility as an author in attempting to address issues of 'race'. I would not pretend to be able to accurately represent black experience. I am especially concious of my inadequacy manifest in my clumsiness and insensitivity of language when attempting to relate the findings of this research and portray the impact of discriminatory practice for Black defendants and their families. I apologise in advance for any offence caused. I am not at all apologetic however, for pursuing the project since I firmly believe that it is the responsibility of white workers to scrutinise their work, to understand the impact it has and to strive to eliminate the racist potential in their practice however unintended it is.

2   Racism

In the course of this chapter I shall give consideration to the place of Black people in Britain. Beginning with reflections on notions of racism, I shall go on to trace the origins of racism within British culture. I will demonstrate how British colonialism engendered ideas of white superiority and how this became translated into racism within post-war Britain. I shall show how any notions of belonging and security within Black communities are undermined from the outset through immigration laws and how racism is re-inforced through the application of legislation. I shall point up how anti-racist and equal opportunity strategies have been developed and identify some respects in which they have failed Black people. Finally, I shall show that anti-racist monitoring needs to be conducted according to frameworks which are not narrowly exclusive but which take account of movement both within and between racial groups and which constitute the basis from which anti-racist and ethnically sensitive services may be accurately targeted.

The emergence of racist Britain

Racism is defined as the belief in the inherent superiority of a particular 'race' over all others, the consequent right to dominate inferior 'races' and the prejudice based on this belief (Lorde, 1984; Oxford English Dictionary, 1990). Cashmore and Troyna (1983) go further in explaining that this doctrine asserts that the population of the world is divided into a range of categories, each category having its own distinctive features. It is argued that these categories may be ordered hierarchically with the result that certain segments of the population are perceived as superior to others. Husband

(1986) points to the irony of a consensual belief in objective categories of 'race' when such notions have been 'virtually buried...beneath the weight of criticism from the international academic community' (p.3).

If racial classification lacks scientific validity, then it follows that supposedly objective assertions of the superiority of one 'race' over another are groundless (Banton and Harwood, 1975). Nevertheless, the lack of scientific support for notions of the right to dominate has done nothing to eliminate racist attitudes and practices within white British society. Hence racism involves prejudice, since it is based upon unreliable, possibly distorted, stereotypical images (Ely and Denney, 1987). What gives continuing impetus to racism in Britain is the legacy of a colonial empire and the subjugation of peoples which has permeated into the self-perception of white British people.

White perceptions of British history have taught that the 'British race' is not only indomitable, having repelled invasion by foreign powers for over a thousand years but is also superior to other 'races', as evidenced through 'conquering' and colonizing other nations. The establishment and maintenance of empire on three continents over several centuries imbued the 'British' with a sense of superiority over other 'races'. Thus, the installation of bureaucracies to administer the colonies was perceived as bringing civilization to 'pagans'. Such ideas were reinforced in the nineteenth century when a scientific basis for racial superiority emerged. Husband (1986) cites the writings of Cuvier and Knox, amongst others, as having justified imperialism as a development of the natural order which protected 'subject races' from themselves and rationalised colonialism as the extension of control from a benign benefactor.

In the twentieth century, as those same 'subject races' wrested independence from the white colonial power, the (white) 'British race' underwent the identity crisis of a superior people without subordinates. This was resolved to some extent by victory over Nazi Germany and found new impetus through the economic growth of the 1950s which brought about the need for an enlarged labour force recruited chiefly from the countries of the Commonwealth. Thus an imperialist framework was recreated within Britain itself (Solomos, 1992).

Immigration control and Black people

As Black immigrant workers took up residence in Britain they were perceived to be both the answer to an economic issue, in that they fulfilled a role in performing tasks within the largely unskilled, low paid work sector, but also as a problem, in that in settling in Britain migrant workers from the Commonwealth were, in theory, entitled to claim the full benefits of citizenship in the form of housing, employment, health care, national assistance, etc. In addition, Black workers wished to be joined by their families and dependants. This was problematic to a people who had belief in their superiority over other 'races' and who had visions of being 'swamped' by an influx of Black people. The recruitment drive of the 1950s was quickly followed, therefore, by legislation designed to make entry into Britain increasingly restrictive, especially to Black workers' partners and dependants.

Successive pieces of immigration legislation have not only enacted increasingly restrictive entry criteria but have also been implemented in ways which undermine existing Black communities. In doing so, it has rendered Black people vulnerable as to their position, future and security in Britain. For example, The Immigration Act 1973 was applied retrospectively and held that those who had entered the country illegally could be deported long after the event, even though previous legislation ruled that they could not. Immigration legislation overturned legal precedent in that, in cases brought before the courts, rulings have been made by judges and Law Lords, i.e. those people conventionally regarded as appointed to be the guardians of the rights of individuals. Further erosion of the rights of individuals were brought about by Appeal Court rulings which applied the law in ways not envisaged by Members of Parliament during the process of enactment (Gordon, 1983). The courts also favoured government agencies in relation to amnesties for illegal immigrants. The Court of Appeal found that such amnesties conferred no rights on the individual but served only to mitigate the effects of the law.

Similar examples of legislation being implemented in such a way as to disadvantage Black people may be found in relation to the rules of appeal, the definition of 'illegal immigrants', detention of people alleged to be 'illegal immigrants' and the application of Habeas Corpus rulings. That the Home Office should believe a person to be an 'illegal immigrant' has proved to be enough, without evidence or the requirement to establish the burden of proof, to deny writs of Habeas Corpus being granted (Gordon, 1983). Such judgements have undermined the security of Black people who understood that they were permanently settled in Britain and has portrayed that Black presence as unwanted and unwelcome. In these and other ways racism has become enshrined in the structure and fabric of British institutions.

Institutional racism

Glasgow (1980) defines institutional racism as the policies of institutions which work to perpetuate racist ideology without acknowledging that fact. This concept is sometimes referred to as 'camouflaged racism' since it is not open and visible but is concealed in the routine practices and procedures of organisations. However, this notion is not universally accepted. Gordon (1990) summarises the stance of the political right which asserts that what exists is not institutional racism but personal racism: the behaviour of individuals who behave in a discriminatory way. The examples quoted earlier of the manner in which immigration law has been applied would suggest that conscious racism - the belief in the superiority of one 'race' over another - became embodied in the functions of institutions, seemingly as a concious and deliberate part of policy. Only more recently, since racism was selectively outlawed under the terms of the Race Relations Act 1976 and institutions developed equal opportunities and anti-racist strategies has the manifestation of racism been less obvious and more ambiguous.

Despite these moves to counter racism there have been widespread examples of institutions continuing to work against the interests of Black people. The very Act designed to bring an end to discrimination on the grounds of 'race' was itself implemented prejudicially. Shortly after the implementation of the Race Relations Act 1976 cases brought to court frequently resulted in judgements favouring the defendants - those allegedly discriminating on the grounds of 'race' - in areas which Griffith (1977) argued the alternative interpretation was clearly available to the courts. In relation to housing issues the 'home' of the Black person was deemed to be the country of origin, not Britain, irrespective of the length of time they had been 'settled' (Gordon, 1983). In other circumstances the powers of the Commission for Racial Equality to investigate alleged discrimination against Black people have been curtailed by the courts allowing racist practices to go unchallenged (Gordon, 1983).

The focus of this study is on discrimination on the grounds of 'race' insofar as it is apparent within the juvenile justice system. In this context too, increasingly widespread concerns have been expressed, particularly in the last decade. The Institute of Race Relations noted:

It is not possible to speak of the rights and liberties of suspected and accused persons without noting at the same time that the whole Black community is suspect - and accused, just of being here...The suspicion of the West Indian [sic] is that he is a criminal, a wild man, emanating from

13

the jungles of Africa via the Caribbean - mixed up with drums and voodoo and dark, dark rites (Cited in Scraton and Gordon, 1984).

The issue of racism in the criminal justice system is discussed at length later. Suffice it to note here that the stereotypical notion of Black people as criminals, vividly portrayed above, is one that has prevailed in the criminal justice arena. It seems possible that just as stereotypical images of women have apparently led to more severe punishment of those women who have offended, there has been a similar process in operation in relation to Black defendants.

Heidensohn (1987) noted that women who appear in court having committed offences are seen to be doubly deviant. In consequence, they are punished first for being in court and again for not conforming to the classic female stereotype. Edwards (1984) echoed the notion of the double punishment of women: first for the crime they had committed and secondly, for the extent to which they deviated from what was regarded as appropriate female behaviour. In both cases the secondary punishment related to the deviation from a perceived positive stereotype embodied in the virtues of motherhood and so on.

Like women, it seems that Black people receive a double punishment from the courts - punished first for the crime - but then, whereas women are punished a second time for deviance from a perceived positive stereotype, Black people are punished a second time for seeming conformity to a negative stereotype. In both cases, the experiences of women and Black people is of discriminatory sentencing.

The impact of anti-racism

The 1980s saw the development of equal opportunity policies and anti-racist strategies most particularly amongst government agencies - central and local - and focused mainly upon public services. The twin features of these policies was equal access to services and employment opportunities and the elimination of discriminatory practices. Amongst those agencies that adopted equal opportunity policies were the health and probation services, local authorities and, most recently, police forces. At the heart of successful implementation of equal opportunities policies was considered to be staff training in 'race' awareness and anti-discriminatory practice (Ball and Solomos, 1990). However, as Gordon (1990) noted, too much that passed for anti-racism or 'race' equality policies left itself open to the kinds of attack that appeared in the press. Local authorities indulged in gestural

14

politics, engaging with appearance rather than dealing with material realities; elevating relatively minor issues to the role of major ones and *vice versa*.

Similarly, Ouseley (1990) identified the neglect of major issues of policy, practice and service provision, with equal opportunity statements appearing to be a gloss on recruitment slogans rather than signifying real intent. Parks and residential homes for older people were re-named after Black cultural heroes whilst ethnically sensitive services were notable by their absence.

In the political climate of the late 1980s and into the 1990s, 'race' equality initiatives were increasingly pushed further down local political agendas. Local authorities were undergoing transition and through such measures as compulsory competitive tendering have become enabling bodies more than direct service providers. In these circumstances oversight of 'race' equality practices has become distanced.

Much of the transition has come about in the face of considerable hostility between largely Labour controlled local government and the Conservative national government. Such has been the ferocity of the confrontation that some local authorities have become absorbed with the need to survive; expediency and damage limitation taking precedence over combating racism. But there has also been opposition to anti-racism from within authorities as well as outside resulting in policies being implemented with a lack of conviction by white staff. At least one local authority experienced a drop in the proportion of Black staff it employed in the year following the implementation of its equal opportunities in recruitment and selection policy.

Amongst those who were genuinely attempting to apply the policies there was a feeling that they would unearth something that they could not deal with (Rutherford, 1992). Lorna Whyte noted:

> When we start talking about issues of 'race', fear is a motivation. It often stops people from doing things. We need a greater understanding of what is happening. People need to get away from the idea that [racism] is all about what individuals do to other individuals and to understand that it is much more likely to be about how systems are operating (Cited in Rutherford, 1992. p.144).

However, local authorities do not operate in a vacuum but are under constant public gaze. Some local authority action which was designed to empower Black communities, promote visible justice and/or protect the interests of racial minorities has provoked considerable reaction from the white majority

(Ouseley, 1990). Witness the reaction of white people to those authorities wishing to demonstrate solidarity with Black people through the public support for and promotion of cultural festivities and organisations. For example, in 1988 Wolverhampton Borough Council wished to defuse tension in the local community by demonstrating support for the Black community and of one family in particular in their pursuit of justice following the death of a Black young adult whilst in the process of being arrested on suspicion of the fraudulent use of a credit card. The death had provoked a strong reaction, especially from Black people, around allegations of the amount of force used during the arrest. Seeking to ensure that justice was seen to be done and to secure the accountability of West Midlands Police to the public the Council offered support to the dead man's family. This gesture provoked considerable adverse reaction from the local white majority which ultimately led, in the opinion of the local press and radio, to the subsequent change in political control of the council in the following elections and to the removal from power of the leader of the Labour group.

I have argued that anti-racism lacked the conviction and support of the white majority resulting in, at best, patchy implementation. Doubts have also been expressed about the very direction and basis of anti-racist strategies. Gilroy (1990) argues that anti-racism, based on definitive and fixed divisions of 'race', is an inappropriate measure since it relies on insurmountable cultural and experiential divisions. It defines people according to fixed 'race' groupings and does not allow for movement between groups or for developments within society. It fails to take account of increasing fluidity and movement between communities through dual heritage relationships. Similarly, it denies the experience of Black people in professional and managerial positions. As such, it is argued, anti-racism is itself, patronisingly stereotypical, employing exclusive definitions and terminology. 'Race' or the racial origin of an individual is not a scientific definition but is socially constructed (Shallice and Gordon, 1990). Anti-racism has taken little account of the self-perception of individuals but has consigned them to externally defined, pre-determined groups.

Whilst these arguments carry some weight they seem not to recognise the 'threshold world' seemingly experienced by many Black people who cross the 'race' divisions. People in cross-cultural relationships have long been targeted for especially adverse attention, as have the children born to these relationships. Similarly, Black people in professional and managerial positions have experienced racism precisely because they have successfully attained these positions and in doing so do not conform to racial stereotypes. Furthermore, outside the working environment they have not been judged as

16

managers and professionals but have had their status denied them by white people, frequently being assumed to have acquired the material benefits of higher status by illegal and/or immoral means. Simultaneously, they have not infrequently been the subject of criticism by Black contemporaries on the presumption of having 'sold out' to the white establishment. The derogatory label of 'coconut' has been used; asserting that the person is 'Black on the outside but white in the middle'. There is a heavy price to be paid in the form of greater exposure to racism by Black people who are in positions of management and/or in trans-racial relationships.

Paradoxically, at the same time that a call goes out for greater recognition of the fluidity and movement in society, systems designed to monitor the effects and experience of racism are demanding greater specificity in defining racial origin. In so doing the identity of those who cross the divides is at risk. Whilst it was valid until relatively recently to group people into three or four ethnic groups, debates arising from the 1991 census and views represented by the Commission for Racial Equality have supported the need for seven or nine groups, thus defining people's perceptions of their racial origins more narrowly.

Nevertheless, in the light of the political discredit of anti-racism, Gilroy's (1990) argument that it is no longer a useful concept is one which requires closer attention. Having failed to eliminate discriminatory practice and create genuine equal opportunities it would be easy to fall into the trap of dispensing with anti-racist strategies altogether. However, to do so would be to play into the hands of the political right who are not sympathetic to anti-racism and may utilise evidence highlighting the ineffectiveness of anti-racist strategies to dispense with the legislation it hinges upon. Instead, it is argued that new strategies are required with the simpler, more focused aim of ending racism. 'Race' and racism are not separate peripheral activities but are intrinsic components within all elements of society and of history as it unfolds.

Whilst anti-racism and equal opportunity strategies have been pitched at the level of generality, there is nonetheless, a need for close scrutiny of outcomes for services users. There is a need, therefore, to retain fewer broad bands of 'race' in order to detect and monitor the effects of racism but to employ a greater number of more specific groupings to ensure the provision of ethnically sensitive services. In view of this observation, for the purposes of this study, which is to detect racism in the form of differential sentencing, three broad bands of 'race' classifications have been employed: Black (African-caribbean), white and Asian.

17

On the grounds that there is no scientific definition of 'race' it would, at one level, seem spurious to make any distinctions between people. Indeed, there are many who advocate the one 'race' philosophy. However, it is apparent that the experiences of people are different and that skin colour is one factor in that difference. To adopt a 'colour-blind' approach, as I have argued, is itself racist in effect, since it denies cultural diversity. More particularly, the 'colour-blind' approach denies the abuse of power which Black people experience daily. Having established the need to acknowledge differences in ethnicity, how is this to be defined? As individuals we have our own self-perceptions of identity. Equally, we are subject to a socially constructed identity, i.e. how other people see us.

I have argued that in connection with the provision of ethnically sensitive services it is important to establish the individual's own definition of their identity in order to most appropriately respond to need. Indeed, in this context, assumptions on the part of the agency about the identity of the individual may lead to inappropriate services being proved and/or to insensitivity in the provision of those services. For the purpose of this study, where the intention is to establish the nature and extent of discriminatory practices, it is important to utilise notions of identity which are imposed on the individual because it is in the assumptions that are made about defendants that discrimination may occur. Furthermore, because the identity is externally defined it is likely to be stereotypical and less sophisticated. Consequently, there is need for fewer definitions or groups of identities.

In the course of this chapter I have shown how from the days of empire and the scientific legitimation of racism, the (white) British 'race' has perceived itself as superior to other 'races'. I have demonstrated that racism became translated into legislation following the demise of the empire and mass immigration and, that the enactment and application of the law has undermined and called into question the very presence of Black people in Britain. I have provided evidence of how institutional racism has permeated agencies and organisations and has curtailed the powers of race relations legislation along with agencies intended to enforce it. I have traced how anti-racism has developed and been discredited by political expediency and lack of conviction by white people. I have presented an alternative framework for detecting and monitoring racism which is sufficiently flexible to accommodate changes in the composition of society but which can be specifically focused to provide for targeting ethnically sensitive services.

In the course of the next chapter I shall trace the development of a separate justice system for juveniles and demonstrate how, both in structure and operation, it has been framed by changing ideologies. I shall argue that in

18

much the same way that Black people have been disadvantaged by institutional racism in British society as a whole, disadvantage has also been apparent in the juvenile justice system as a result of the 'colour-blindness' of the ideologies that have shaped it.

3 Changing ideologies and the development of the juvenile justice system in England and Wales

In the previous chapter I traced the origins of racism in contemporary British society from the justification of the Empire through the belief in the innate superiority of the (white) British 'race' over conquered Black 'races'. I showed that even after such doctrines were discredited by the international academic community, white British people continued to believe in their own innate superiority which was translated into institutional racism within the infrastructure. I produced evidence of the manifestation of institutional racism, primarily through the implementation and application of immigration and race relations legislation. Finally, I demonstrated how attempts at anti-racism had been undermined and discussed the need for a bifurcated approach which allows for racism to be monitored using a more flexible and less exclusive model of society but which is sufficiently specific to facilitate the targeting of ethnically sensitive services.

In the first part of this chapter I shall trace the development of changing ideologies in relation to juvenile offending as reflected in, or prompted by, social policy. I shall show that juvenile crime is not a new phenomenon - in spite of what the media would have us believe - and that alongside concerns shown by some groups of people about the treatment of juvenile offenders, both in the courts and in penal institutions, tensions have continued to exist in relation to determining the most effective response to juvenile crime. Through reference to legislation and committee reports I shall show how emphasis on the welfare needs of children and young people in trouble emerged and culminated in an ideological debate played out in the juvenile justice system. I shall show how that debate produced unintended and unexpected consequences which, combined with new directions in government policy, have produced dual and increasingly convergent ideologies through the 1980s; one led by social policy and the other arising out of juvenile justice practice. However, I shall argue that ideologies have failed to take 'race' into account and have contributed to discriminatory practices.

In the second part of the chapter I shall outline the principles and operation of the tariff system within the legislative context that applied at the time of the study and discuss the relative merits of the cases for and against its existence. I shall show how the tariff impacted upon notions of 'individualised' and tariff sentencing and consider some of the issues arising from ideological stances in relation to the tariff system. Although notions of a sentencing tariff were significantly affected by s.29(2) of the Criminal Justice Act 1991 which effectively forbade consideration of previous sentencing outcomes when considering what disposal to impose in response to the current offences, the effects of that section have since been overturned through subsequent legislation and the situation as it applied in 1990 is largely that which applies today. This makes the discussion about the impact and effects of tariff sentencing all the more important, especially insofar as it affects Pre-sentence Report practice.

Concerns about juvenile crime

In his study into historical public perceptions of juvenile crime and the morals of the young, Geoffrey Pearson (1983) began by looking at contemporary expressions of concern arising from popular perceptions of relentlessly increasing juvenile crime and found that there were echoes to be found in each generation, going back through British history for over four hundred years. In the Report of the Society for the Improvement of Prison Discipline and for the Reformation of Juvenile Offenders, 1818, it was stated that:

> Juvenile delinquency has, of late years, increased to an unprecedented extent, and is still rapidly and progressively increasing (Cited in, Morris and Giller, 1987, p. 56).

It is apparent, therefore, that juvenile crime is not a new phenomenon and that concerns about the offending behaviour of children and young people have existed for many years. Whilst those concerns have been widely held and frequently voiced (Pearson, 1983) the most effective way of responding to juvenile crime has been the subject of on-going debate.

Prior to 1908, adult and juvenile offenders were subject to the same justice system. Although there was an element of welfarism in the judicial principle

21

of diminished responsibility by virtue of age, the major emphasis of the courts when dealing with child offenders was to bring to bear the full range of sentencing options, up to and including the death penalty, in just deserts for the offence committed (Paley and Thorpe, 1980). Indeed, it was reported that on one day in 1814 five children between the ages of eight and 12 years were hanged for petty larceny (Pinchbeck and Hewitt, 1973).

The operation of the justice system at this time was firmly based upon the principles of a 'justice' ideology: that is to say, an assertion that crime is freely entered into by offenders and is consequently an immoral act against social rules enshrined in the law which is the institutional representation of a moral consensus within society (Parsloe, 1976; Bean, 1976; Adams et al, 1981). Furthermore, it is asserted that delinquent behaviour is learned, rational and arises out of a concious decision making process (Wiggin, 1981).

The rationale of the 'justice' model is to protect the community through the detection of crime and the punishment of offenders. It is no coincidence then, that the origins of the modern police force designed to detect crime, apprehend offenders and bring them to justice are found in this period in history. To ensure that justice is administered, the rights of the offender are safeguarded and protected by rules of due process, including the right to legal representation. Punishment, rather than revenge or treatment, is the sole object of the 'justice' model; imposed in order to achieve retribution for the offence(s) committed and to deter further offending, both by the individual sentenced as well as other potential offenders. The punishment, which is imposed on behalf of society, is of determinate length or scale and is in proportion to the offence(s) committed (Bean, 1976; Parsloe, 1976; Adams et al, 1981; Wiggin, 1981).

The origins of the juvenile justice system

The Philanthropic Society consistently advocated greater use of the judicial principle of diminished responsibility and, highlighting the link between age and deprivation, argued that these factors should mitigate against the full use of penal sanctions for child offenders (Paley and Thorpe, 1980). Others began to express concern that the incarceration of children in penal institutions alongside adults had a contaminating effect from which they should be protected. For example, in 1836, Inspectors of Prisons reported:

> ...the boy is thrown among veterans in guilt...and his vicious propensities cherished and inflamed...He enters the prison, a child in years, and not

also infrequently, in crime: but he leaves it with a knowledge in the ways of wickedness (Cited in Morris and Giller, 1987, p. 59).

In social policy terms, the watershed for dealing with juvenile offenders as a separate entity from adults came about through the enactment of the Children Act 1908. This move was based on the premise that children in poorer areas were neglected and abused (Morris and Giller, 1987). For their protection therefore, confidential court proceedings were to be heard in newly created juvenile courts with powers to impose education and training through Borstal Institutions. In this respect, Magistrates were required to establish the need for care of the juvenile and, where necessary, to enforce removal from home. This Act abolished imprisonment for those under 14 years old and restricted prison sentences for 14-16 year olds.

It was apparent through this legislation that the beginnings of a welfare need-centred approach were being laid down. The abolition of custody for the youngest offenders and its restricted use for the older age group removed the cornerstone of 'justice' model punishment and introduced notions of 'treatment' and reform through semi-determinate Borstal Training sentences. The link between deprivation and delinquency was cemented through jurisdiction in cases relating to the care and neglect of children being heard in the same juvenile courts alongside criminal matters.

Whilst the emergence of this need-centred approach brought with it the abolition of penal sentencing for the youngest offenders, the welfare response was no less punitive in effect since it too relied upon the removal of children from their homes and families. Whether the purpose of removal is for punishment or treatment purposes is immaterial to the child concerned, it is the removal that is significant. Worse still, the period of removal under this welfare regime was only semi-determinate; under the previous system the length of sentence was an absolute from the outset and, however, unpalatable, was a known entity.

The growth of 'welfarism'

Having established the principle of separate juvenile courts, there followed a period of reinforcement and consolidation through a number of measures. The Moloney Committee, reporting in 1927, brought about the introduction of juvenile benches comprising specially selected Magistrates who would have a caring concern for juveniles, an awareness of their interests and an understanding of the difficulties they face. However, Moloney, recommended the retention of the 'justice' model notion of delinquents

23

being responsible for their own actions and of lawbreaking being concious and deliberate. Furthermore, the Committee expressed the view that there was a need to retain the formal processes of the court in order to communicate the seriousness with which anti-social behaviour was viewed. Nonetheless, there was recognition that juveniles who committed offences were themselves victims of social and psychological conditions beyond their control: factors which should mitigate against recourse to the full range of sentencing (HMSO, 1927). In this recognition may be traced the initial emergence of a more welfarist approach to juvenile offenders which would gain momentum over the next 40 years.

The link between neglect and delinquency made evident in the Moloney Report underpinned the provisions of the Children and Young Persons Act as it was consolidated in the following year. The main principle of the legislation was that courts would have regard to the welfare of the juvenile when determining what sentence to impose. To this end, the courts were empowered to request Social Inquiry Reports (SIRs) to assist them in making an assessment of the juvenile's welfare needs (see chapter 4). In addition, to further equip the courts to address educational and welfare needs, courts were empowered to order residence at an Approved School.

'Welfare' and state provision

The emergence of the 'welfare' principle gained momentum in harness with the establishment of the welfare state in the 1940s and 1950s. The Children Act 1948, based on the findings of the Curtis Committee, enabled local authorities to take children considered to be in need of care and protection and assume the powers and duties of parents and led to creation of Children's Departments. In the same year, through the provisions of the Criminal Justice Act, some of the more punitive sentencing options - corporal punishment and imprisonment for under 17s - were abolished. In their place Detention and Attendance Centres were introduced. Whilst these measures incorporated 'justice' model principles of retribution through determinate periods of loss of liberty, the emphasis was on providing a secure, structured regime, designed to build character. They were, therefore, as much to address need through the provision of education and training as they were to instil discipline (Morris and Giller, 1987).

Concurrent with these measures, the Atlee government was putting into place the pillars of the welfare state through the creation of the National Health Service, National Assistance and comprehensive changes in education provision. These developments reflected the social democratic ideology of the age, manifest in a supposedly benevolent welfare state, increasing the scope of the state to provide for the needs of children and families (Adams et al, 1981).

Within ten years, however, shortcomings in welfare state provision began to emerge. Access to higher education proved largely impenetrable to working class youth. The National Health Service reforms proved to have paid little attention to the needs of people with mental health problems or learning difficulties and the National Assistance Board had failed to mop up the residue of need in the way it was originally anticipated. Similarly, increased service provision for children and families was perceived to have failed to assist 'dysfunctional families' whilst levels of juvenile crime did not diminish (Adams et al, 1981; Morris and Giller, 1987; Paley and Thorpe, 1980).

Delinquency and deprivation

In response to growing calls for government action to address the perceived mounting tide of juvenile delinquency (Pearson, 1983) the Ingleby Committee was established in 1956 with a brief to examine the operation and effectiveness of the juvenile justice system. It was here that the direct link between child neglect and delinquency first came under close scrutiny and that the notion of preventing neglect as a means of addressing delinquency was articulated as a serious concept (Evans, 1982). Reporting in 1960, the Committee laid emphasis on the lack of any noticeable difference in the character and needs of the neglected when compared with those the delinquent child. It identified unsatisfactory homes as the common source of both crime and neglect and proposed new powers to prevent or forestall the suffering of children through neglect in their own homes (Morris and Giller, 1987) by supporting the provision of housing, health education and welfare services to families who were deemed to be 'at risk' (HMSO, 1960).

Whereas the findings of the Ingleby Committee might easily have led to the conclusion that the welfare state was flawed to the point where it had become untenable, instead it was proposed that the existing blanket of state provision should be superimposed with additional provision directed at those families who, in some way, had slipped through the net of mainstream services. It would be a further 20 years before the concept of the welfare state itself would be seriously challenged.

The Ingleby Report concluded that the welfare and justice functions of the juvenile justice system were irreconcilable. Justice, as a means of responding to juvenile crime focused upon offending behaviour in isolation from the character and needs of the juvenile. Conversely, responding to welfare need depended on a complex of personal, family and social considerations which mitigated against notions of culpability.

The Committee also recognised that sentencing primarily on the grounds of welfare considerations had the potential for disposals to be imposed which may be disproportionate to the seriousness of the offence (Paley and Thorpe, 1980). In highlighting this issue, the Committee were amongst the first to recognise that the commission of a relatively minor offence by a child may lead to the discovery of significant welfare need. Whereas a response which reflected the petty nature of the offence may lead to the imposition of a low-tariff sentence (say, a fine or a discharge), the welfare needs may warrant a significantly more intrusive and higher tariff court order. However, these observations went unheeded in framing subsequent legislation and not until the 1970s were the implications recognised in practice.

In spite of the focus on the link between delinquency and deprivation and the proposals to address offending through additional, targeted welfare provision, the Ingleby Report argued for the retention of juvenile courts on the grounds that issues of personal liberty required the proper protection and safeguards afforded by those purportedly operating with the welfare of the juvenile in mind. Once again, the impact of this argument was not recognised and only discovered in practice in the 1970s when the liberty of many children and young people was taken away at the discretion of social workers.

It was recognised in the Report however, that there was a need to remove the youngest offenders from the juvenile justice system. In order to do this it was proposed to raise the age of criminal responsibility in two stages: initially to 12 years of age and ultimately to14. For children under the age of criminal responsibility it was proposed that care and protection procedures were implemented in order that their welfare needs might be met. In making this proposal, however, the principle of safeguarding the rights of the child through due process of law were arguably compromised.

In attempting to reconcile the irreconcilable the effect of the Ingleby recommendations therefore, would be to retain a formal juvenile justice system based upon 'justice' principles operating alongside reinforced welfare-centred provision. Simultaneously, the personal culpability issue would be removed from the youngest offenders who would be diverted away from the justice system towards welfare provision.

In spite of the efforts to wrestle with the tensions arising from the need for justice but also of responding to unmet welfare needs, the recommendations of the Ingleby Committee were not fully adopted. The age of criminal responsibility was raised in the Children and Young Persons Act 1963 but only to ten years of age. Most crucially, the measures designed to address welfare needs were not adopted. Local authorities were, however, given enabling powers, not least in relation to provision required to avoid the need to remove children from their homes. Where removal could be averted through the provision of preventive services or financial assistance to address specific and usually, short-term problems, local authorities were given powers to respond.

The 'welfare' model

It was at this point in time that the 'welfare' model became increasingly significant within the debate on how best to respond to juvenile crime. It is appropriate here, therefore, to outline the principles of the 'welfare' model before going on to consider the growing impact of 'welfarism' on subsequent developments in social policy.

Davies (1980) describes 'welfarism' as a particular configuration of theories and beliefs which fit together in a complex and untidy way (Cited in, Evans, 1982). Based on the principles of 'welfarism' as identified by Davies (1980) and Adams et al (1981), Evans outlines three main features of the 'welfare' model.

First, 'welfarism is centred on a selective definition of social problems, namely those amenable to solution by the intervention of state agencies which are aimed at achieving the reform or rehabilitation of the offender. In this context, notions of class are crucially relevant since within the model 'youthful crime' is perceived to arise from certain types of working class families.

Secondly, it is focused upon family pathology. 'Youthful crime', it is argued, is a product of certain unrespectable working class families who have been failed by the welfare state or who have themselves failed to take up the opportunities the welfare state offers. Delinquency, then, is seen as a manifestation of a broader problem, namely deprivation. Davies (1980) identifies the family as the primary agent for socialising the young but in working class families there are perceived to be few rewards for such socialisation. However, society relies upon a successful socialisation process for the reproduction of labour and so, when the family fails to socialise its young, state intervention is necessary to undertake the process (Davies 1980, cited in, Evans, 1982).

The 'welfarist' focus on family pathology also draws on interactionist labelling theory in drawing attention to the unequal treatment the children of working class receive in response to their misconduct in comparison with middle and upper class children. A consequence of this unequal treatment is stigmatisation arising from involvement in the juvenile justice system and the acquisition of a criminal record.

'Welfarists' take the view that since delinquency arises from certain identifiable types of family, it is possible, in advance, to predict which families will 'produce' delinquents and then to engage those children in preventive intervention. However, such preventive intervention carries risks in the form of producing self-fulfilling prophecies perpetuated by net-widening insofar as it fails to recognise the stigmatisation of labelling brought about through the involvement of state agencies with families.

Effective preventive intervention is dependent upon accurate prediction of who is 'at risk'. The 'welfare' model places a high offending risk factor on deprivation. It is clear though, that many children experience deprivation but do not go on to display offending behaviour. A further qualification of deprived families is required to determine which are likely to 'produce' children who will offend. The 'welfare' model defines these as unrespectable working class families. However, respectability and unrespectability are not objective concepts and require subjective value judgements to be made to determine which children are 'at risk' of offending and which are not. This in itself may lead to a 'scatter-gun' approach to the provision of preventive services. In addition, the desire to 'protect' children from the risk of offending may result in the liberal application of any test for unrespectability.

Furthermore, to determine that a family is unrespectable and their children are 'at risk' of offending is to apply a stigmatising label which becomes conspicuous to the community through the provision of preventive services. Thus, a model which is designed to avoid the stigmatising effect of the labelling process that is an inevitable consequence of a child's involvement in the juvenile justice system has the unintended effect of creating labelling through the involvement of state welfare services (Taylor, Walton and Young, 1973, p. 112).

Arguably, the negative effects of labelling brought about through preventive work may be more significant since, in order to attain the label of 'delinquent' the child only needs to be in receipt of a service having been deemed to be 'at risk' of offending. On the other hand, the label that is applied as a result of a court appearance is reliant, at least, upon an allegation of an offence being made.

The third feature of 'welfarism' identified by Evans (1982) is its concern to locate delinquency causation and control within the working class community. This reflects the emphasis placed on 'community' or 'neighbourhood' as:

1. The creator and sustainer of delinquency.

2. The vehicle for the provision of services.

3. The natural environment for life and the assessment of behaviour (Evans, 1982, p. 9).

Other writers have revealed additional facets of the 'welfare' model. Wiggin (1981) sees treatment on a medical model as the response of 'welfarism' to juvenile offending based on the principle of change from within the individual. The measures that are imposed aim towards the accomplishment of change (De May, 1971) and because these measures take the form of treatment, not punishment, there is no need for determinate sentences (Wiggin, 1981). Indeed, it is argued that indeterminate sentences are necessary in order to allow sufficient flexibility to respond to progress and changing circumstances. However, Wilson (Cited in Wiggin, 1981, p. 7) argues that welfare measures must be seen as punitive since there would otherwise be no moral justification for compulsory intervention.

'Welfarists' believe it unnecessary to directly address offending behaviour since it is a symptom of dysfunction and, as such, it is irrelevant. It is said that children from deprived homes need differential provision from children of other backgrounds just as they would if they had not offended (Christie, 1974).

As well as drawing on labelling theory, the 'welfare' model makes use of two other theories; one in relation to the causes of crime, the other focusing upon response to offending - Matza's theory of 'drift' and Schur's notion of 'radical non-intervention. Matza (1964) in developing the theory of drift, began with a consideration of juvenile delinquency. However, his starting point was not 'why do people become delinquent?' Instead he turned the question on its head and asked 'why do people not become delinquent?' He observed that it was the strength or weakness of the bonds to conventional society that determined delinquency. Positive feelings towards authority, he noted, represent the first line of social control but the withdrawal or absence of these positive feelings has the effect of neutralising the moral force of that control. Matza argued that increased police suspicion and activity has the effect of increasing misconduct and pointed to the different responses of localities to differing types and levels of police activity as evidence.

The 'welfare' model extends this theory to include the impact of the justice system as a whole. Just as increased police activity encourages misconduct so too, it is felt, does the activity of the juvenile justice system as a whole. Consequently, it is argued that if this activity could be curtailed or diminished, so misconduct would be reduced. Home Secretary David (later Lord) Waddington made a similar point when addressing a meeting of the Howard League for Penal Reform in 1990, which I attended, in saying that whilst it was important to respond to juvenile offending it was more important not to overreact since to do so potentially contains the inherent danger of stimulating further offending.

This theory of delinquency has also provided 'welfarists' with a criticism of the 'justice' model. The emphasis of 'justice' on the detection of crime and punishment of offenders, according to 'welfare' theory, is counter-productive to the aim of reducing criminal activity. Instead, the attempt to deter, punish and prevent criminal acts can itself stimulate deviance (Taylor, Walton and Young, 1973) Pearson argues that the justice lobby has:

> created a self-fulfilling prophesy, which generates, by its tougher attitude in the material practice of law enforcement, increased crime statistics, and then uses those same statistics to get tough in order to arrest the downward spiral (Pearson, 1978, p. 14).

Schur's concept of 'radical non-intervention' (Schur, 1971) is that without the over-reaction of society, 'youthful delinquency' will pass away. However, Rutherford (1992) directs this same criticism at the 'welfare' model and points to the increased loss of liberty on welfare grounds being frequently incommensurate with the seriousness of the offence committed.

The 'welfare' model is based upon a process of diagnosis and treatment: de-emphasising the delinquent act and focusing instead on the underlying attitude, relationships and family of the delinquent. The families where deprivation exists are regarded as 'crimogenic'. That is to say, the potential for crime exists irrespective of whether or not an offence has been committed. Those who focus upon decriminalisation and decarceration claim that both prosecution and custody are not only ineffective methods of dealing with delinquency but are themselves capable of generating delinquent careers and, in so doing, perpetuate delinquency.

'Justice', 'welfare' and mass immigration

Mass immigration began in the mid-1950s. Until then the population of Britain was essentially 'white'. Since the foundations of 'justice' had been established several decades earlier it was clearly based on mono-cultural principles even though there has been a Black presence in Britain for many centuries. Similarly, the progression to a more 'welfare' orientated juvenile justice system also pre-dates mass immigration. The impact of 'race' and Black experience were consequently absent from these ideologies. Indeed, 'welfarism' was founded on notions of disparity on the basis of social class.

The experience of Black people has been long in being recognised and not until the early 1980s did those differential experiences of the justice system begin to be acknowledged. Not until the weight of anecdotal evidence of the over-representation of Black people in custody became overwhelming was it regarded necessary by the Home Office to collate and publish statistics relating to the racial composition of the prison population.

Ideologies themselves seem to be some time in the making and appear less based on contemporary societal conditions than theories that 'grow' and develop over many years. It is apparent, therefore, that the more recent emergence of 'system intervention' and 'corporatism' ideologies (see below), although post-dating mass immigration, do not include any explicit consideration of 'race'. In the absence of 'race' in any ideology, the over-representation of Black people in all sectors of the youth justice system requires that new concepts are developed which address Black experience and institutional racism.

The embodiment of 'welfare' principles in social policy

To return to the historical context then, 'welfarism', as an ideology was enthusiastically adopted by the Labour Party which, in 1964, established a committee chaired by Lord Longford, as a response to the failure of the previous administration to adopt all the recommendations of the Ingleby Committee. The Longford Committee adopted the stance that delinquent acts were committed by dependent victims of circumstance who were consequently in need of therapy and treatment rather than punishment. Radical changes were proposed relating to the way society should respond to juvenile offending, including the abolition of the juvenile courts.

The underlying principle of the Longford Report was that juvenile offending is the product of inequality within society. Delinquency was seen as evidence of the lack of care, guidance and opportunity to which every child was entitled. The juvenile justice system itself was seen as inequitable since it focused on the children of working class families who were drawn into the system whilst those of other classes were perceived to be dealt with without recourse to the courts. The intent of the report's recommendations was to provide working class families with the type of care, guidance and opportunity that was felt to be generally available within other social classes.

The Longford Report recommendations formed the basis of the subsequent White Paper, 'The Child, The Family and The Young Offender', which proposed the replacement of the juvenile court by a Family Council. In this setting the child, in company with her/his parent(s), social workers and other people deemed to have appropriate expertise, would identify particular areas of dysfunction and deprivation in the child's life and circumstances and agree a plan of action to address those issues. In those cases where agreement could not be reached or where the facts of the matter were disputed there was provision for referral to a Family Court hearing.

Failure to secure the paramountcy of 'welfare'

These recommendations enshrined many of the principles of the 'welfare' model: removal of the stigmatisation of a court appearance, notions of family pathology and intervention based on treatment to rectify dysfunction, treatment plans based on consensus and co-operation rather than compulsion, etc. However, the White Paper met with considerable opposition, much of which related to the perceived concentration on 'welfare' principles to the exclusion of notions of justice, particularly with regard to the absence of legal protection and safeguards for the interests of the child. Without the dispassionate objectivity of the legal system, it was argued, the proposals created too many opportunities for the abuse of power (Morris and Giller, 1987). Decisions about the personal liberty of juveniles should not reside solely with social workers.

The combination of considerable opposition to the proposals contained in the White Paper and an insufficient majority to ensure translation into legislation led the Wilson government to a decision not to formulate a Bill. Instead, a second White Paper entitled 'Children in Trouble' was published in 1968. 'Children in Trouble' contended that juvenile offending had 'no single cause, manifestation or cure': a statement which represented a considerable shift in thinking from the principle contained in the Longford Report.

It proposed that under-14s would not be tried for criminal matters but would be subject only to care and protection proceedings on the grounds of welfare need. In doing so, it echoed the Ingleby Committee of twelve years earlier. Offending alone would be insufficient grounds for a court appearance. Instead, children would be dealt with on a voluntary basis. Fourteen to 17 year olds, on the other hand, would continue to be subject to criminal proceedings but only after consultation between police and social workers.

'Children in Trouble' presented a model of juvenile justice which was to be retained within the legal system but with a clear concentration upon informal, rather than formal, action (Morris and Giller, 1987). Care Orders would replace Approved School and Fit Person Orders, implementation of which would be at the discretion of the local authority. Local authorities would also establish community homes with education. Intermediate Treatment would be introduced - operating in the context of Supervision Orders - and would replace Detention and Attendance Centres. The form that Intermediate Treatment should take would be at the discretion of the supervising social worker.

Having failed through the previous White Paper to abolish the juvenile justice system, the intention of 'Children in Trouble' was apparently to dismantle its punitive elements and replace them with measures designed to address need from a 'welfare' perspective. The welfare of the child would be the paramount, if not the only consideration upon which intervention would be based.

As with 'The Child, The Family and The Young Offender', 'Children in Trouble' was not well received in spite of its concession to retain the juvenile court system. Having a larger parliamentary majority than in 1965, however, the Labour government was better equipped to secure its passage through the various stages to enactment (Bottoms, 1984). However, between enactment and implementation the Labour government lost power, being replaced by a Heath government committed to implement only those sections of the Children and Young Persons Act 1969 which it did not oppose. Consequently, the age of criminal responsibility was retained at ten; the police/social worker liaison process was not implemented; Detention and Attendance Centres were retained as was the minimum age of 15 for Borstal training. The result was a juvenile justice system operating on the basis of both 'justice' and 'welfare' models simultaneously.

'Welfare' and 'justice' in an uneasy marriage

The effect of these changes was to create a bifurcated system of juvenile justice with measures designed to address welfare need operating in parallel with punitive, 'justice' model measures. The welfare needs of the offender would not be paramount although there remained the requirement for Magistrates to take them into account when determining what sentence to impose. As a result, even greater tensions were generated between the competing principles of 'welfare' and 'justice' models; principles which the Ingleby Committee had resolved were irreconcilable.

There was no single, clear vision of what the juvenile justice system was attempting to do. Was it there to punish young offenders who wilfully broke the moral consensus and who needed to be deterred from further offending by the imposition of a determinate sentence? Or alternatively, was it there to diagnose deprivation, prescribe the appropriate therapy in the form of an indeterminate order (not punishment) not necessarily related to the scale of the offence(s) but to be revoked at the discretion of the social worker dependent upon the progress attained or a change in circumstances?

As a result of the vacuum that was created by the lack of clear social policy, an uneasy marriage emerged embodying the principles of both the liberal, reform-based philosophy of individualized intervention on the one hand and that of just deserts on the other. This served to bring into being a justice system with in-built conflict which was to result in a problematic justice process producing dissatisfaction amongst many whose task it was to administer the system. Throughout the 1970s, suspicion and distrust was engendered through a process whereby both 'welfarists' and the 'justice' lobby competed with each other in their respective attempts to seize power and control within the system and ultimately determine its direction. Whilst this was all being acted out in court hearings, children and their families looked on in bewilderment, knowing only that they would ultimately be the losers.

The failings of the 1969 Act

The failings of the Children and Young Persons Act 1969, as it was implemented, hinge on this attempt by default to combine principles of 'welfare' and 'justice' within the same system. In addition, though imposition of the supposedly non-coercive but nevertheless controlling intervention of state agencies and provision also proved to have problematic effects. Concerns were expressed that treatment programmes did not succeed

34

in their intended aims of re-habilitating or reforming the offender. Through the comparison of re-offending rates it was asserted that treatment fared slightly worse than fines and was on a par with conditional discharges in reducing offending (HMSO, 1980).

Further criticism of 'welfare' sanctions were associated with the discretion given to social workers together with the indeterminate length of sentences which, it was said, denied offenders of their fundamental rights (Wiggin, 1981). The discretion of social workers had led to the failure of one of the principles of the 'welfare' model in that whilst the community was perceived by 'welfarism' as the natural place for the assessment and treatment of dysfunction, large numbers of juveniles were removed from the community for these purposes. Most importantly, the 'welfare' model, as it was operated in practice, did not take into account the perceptions of the consumers and spectators of the juvenile justice system, namely children their families, the media and the community at large. Thus, although it was a function of the courts to impose 'welfare' measures the perceptions of the onlookers were that the courts were in place to administer justice, which custom and practice determined was punitive.

This led to a variety of perceptions based on the perspective of the individual. 'Welfare' measures carried greater stigmatisation than a custodial or punitive sentence for offenders since it entailed the loss of face and credibility with peers arising out of the allocation of their case to a social worker. 'Justice' model sentences, on the other hand, whilst stigmatising amongst the establishment, carried a degree of kudos amongst the deviant peer group. Consequently, 'welfare' orientated measures frequently received less than wholehearted compliance by offenders.

Parents may experience a mixture of emotions. Whilst the absence of a custodial sentence might be greeted with relief, the involvement of social workers implied a judgement that they were unable to manage their own family affairs which may lead to a loss of standing in the community. The media and the wider community often regarded anything less than a custodial sentence as a 'let off'. The headline, 'youth walks free from court', typically followed the imposition of a non-custodial sentence which is seen as the vanguard of deterrent sentencing.

Unintended consequences

During the early 1970s, after the implementation of the Children and Young Persons Act 1969, a number of unexpected sentencing trends began to emerge. Between 1969 and 1974 the number of supervision orders imposed fell by 20%. In the same period, the number of Detention Centre Orders doubled whilst Borstal Training Orders increased threefold (Home Office Statistics, 1970, 1975). When combined with the increase in the number of juveniles in local authority care subject to s.7(7) Care Orders it is apparent that in this period more juveniles lost their liberty as a consequence of the 1969 Act. Paley and Thorpe (1980) have observed that these increases cannot be explained by increases in rates of juvenile offending.

The concern was expressed that social work practice was leading to loss of liberty. Mistrust by Magistrates in the preparedness of social workers to exercise their discretion in ways which the courts would approve led to greater use of custodial options where there was doubt about the sentence being carried out in the way the courts intended.

Paradoxically, it is apparent that at this time, social workers were exercising their discretionary powers with considerable enthusiasm and zeal. Far from returning children home, which is what Magistrates feared, social workers were in fact exercising their discretion to detain children in institutions. The result was that many juveniles on s.7(7) Care Orders lost their liberty through removal from home and placement in local authority community homes for assessment and treatment (Morris and Giller, 1987). This process was reinforced by the willingness of social workers to recommend Care Orders on 'welfarist' principles in circumstances where the offences themselves were relatively minor and would not warrant a custodial sentence (Paley and Thorpe, 1980).

The notion that 'kindly' social workers would be 'soft' on offenders by exercising their discretion not to implement orders imposed by the court were found to be largely false. To the contrary, as the Ingleby Committee had warned, there seemed to be little regard for the gravity and consequences of removal from home. However, because community home regimes were perceived to be benevolent and the assessment and treatment programmes were regarded as in the interests of the child, removal from home was not equated with loss of liberty. Alternatively, it was perceived as a small but necessary price the child would need to pay for the long term benefits to be gained through the process of reform.

Nevertheless, the myth that social workers were 'soft on crime' was perpetuated and in the face of a rising tide of crime which they felt powerless to halt, Magistrates increasingly imposed custodial sentences (Morris and Giller, 1987) and social workers continued the use of community homes. It was this increased use and resultant cost of residential accommodation that eventually led to the operation of the juvenile justice system in England and Wales coming under the close scrutiny of the House of Commons Expenditure Committee in 1975. The Committee's enquiries led to a total of 40 recommendations being made, including those which placed authority back into the hands of the courts in removing much social work discretion.

From a variety of perspectives the Children and Young Persons Act 1969, together with the 'welfare' model were perceived to have failed (Smith, 1985). Social workers began to acknowledge that 'welfarism' and the increased infringements of liberty had had the unintended consequence of perpetuating and sustaining the offending behaviour of many juveniles, whilst others who had not originally been offenders had drifted into criminal activity through contact with offenders in care establishments or through preventive schemes. Practitioners in Intermediate Treatment agencies began to identify and voice concerns about the stigmatising effect of labelling and recognised that in many cases preventive initiatives with children and young people who had been deemed to be 'at risk' of offending often did not prevent the risk but seemed to increase it whilst simultaneously taking away the Intermediate Treatment Order as a sentencing response. Magistrates argued that since an offender had been undergoing a voluntary preventive Intermediate Treatment programme without eliminating the risk, what purpose was served by imposing a statutory Intermediate Treatment Order? In consequence, new approaches were required which would be more specifically targeted at the serious, persistent offender who was at real risk of custodial sentencing. Such preventive work that continued was passed over to other agencies independent of the juvenile justice system who would be free of the labelling process to operate in a non-targeted way.

The Scottish juvenile justice system

Although the focus of this study is the juvenile justice system in England and Wales it is worthwhile at this point making some comparisons with the development of the neighbouring system in Scotland, beginning in the 1960s.

The Kilbrandon Committee, reporting in 1964, made recommendations similar to those contained in 'The Child, The Family and The Young Offender' but specifically relating to the Scottish juvenile justice system (Adams et al, 1981). These recommendations became enacted in the Social Work (Scotland) Act 1968 which led to the incorporation of the Probation Service into local authority Social Work Departments. The Act created a system of juvenile justice based on Children's Panels comprising lay people with knowledge and/or experience of children and the circumstances in which they live.

Referral to the panel may, in the first instance, only be made with the consent of the juvenile and their parents. In circumstances where matters are disputed cases are brought for hearing in the Sheriff's Court before a judge. Only if the offence is proved may it be referred back to the Children's Panel. The Reporter convenes the Children's Panel and determines whether the case may be dealt with informally by any of the three agencies: Police, Education or Social Work Department. Alternatively, the Reporter may decide, following consideration of reports on the matter, that the juvenile should either be brought before the panel or, that the case may be dealt with by way of a letter or interview indicating the possible consequences of further offending.

The panel is not a legal hearing and so juveniles do not need to be legally represented unless they wish to be. Instead, they may appoint a representative of their choice to accompany them and their parents. The panel, comprising three lay people, may have access to a report prepared by a social worker. Essentially, the panel has two options available when dealing with offenders: a) to discharge the offender or, b) to impose a supervision order. Additional conditions may be attached to the order relating to the juvenile's place of residence and involvement in particular activities. supervision orders are reviewed annually or on request. If agreement cannot be reached about the course of action to be taken the case may be referred to the Sheriff's Court for appeal.

The Scottish system closely resembles that which was proposed in 'The Child, The Family and The Young Offender' and is clearly based on 'welfare' principles. It operates outside the legal system but with the safeguard of reference to the Sheriff's Court in proving the offence and hearing appeals. Further safeguards are afforded to those juveniles who are on supervision orders through the annual review and review on request provisions.

It is interesting to note how the legislation to establish the Scottish system was successfully conducted through parliament and implemented prior to the demise of the Wilson government. As a result of being implemented in the form originally conceived without the confusion of two competing ideologies impacting upon each other as happened in England and Wales, the Scottish system has escaped the controversy and intensity of the 'welfare' versus 'justice' debate as it has been played out in England and Wales.

It may be precisely because the Scottish system was solely based on 'welfare' principles that it has survived largely untouched since it was established. Indeed, it is a matter of some conjecture whether the absence of tension from competing ideologies has prevented the system from falling into discredit as occurred with the system in England and Wales. It begs the question what might have happened had a system been adopted in England and Wales with the same exclusive 'welfare' focus?

Return to 'justice'

Events in England and Wales together with the perceived failure of the 1969 Act led to a missed opportunity for the 'welfare' model and to the resurgence of the 'justice' model as the predominant ideology in the operation of the juvenile justice system. This resurgence coincided with the election of the Thatcher government in 1979 which was not only committed to 'law and order' but also simultaneously to 'rolling back state intervention and reducing public expenditure'. By this time over 6,500 juveniles were annually sentenced to custody (Home Office Statistics, 1979). Action was felt necessary both to reduce the cost implications and increase the range of punitive non-custodial sentencing options available to the courts.

The 'justice' model of the late 1970s and 1980s took on a new philosophical stance which became variously known as 'back to justice', 'return to justice' or 'new justice realism'. Adams et al (1981) identified two radical positions with the new movement. The first espoused the principle of protecting children's rights by:

1. tightening the rules of due process to avoid the possibility of harsh or unjust sentencing.

2. the removal of virtually all social work discretion.

The second stance taken by what Cohen (1985) calls 'disillusioned liberals', serves to unmask the real effects of the 'welfare' model in order to reveal that things done to children in the pursuit of reform through treatment may actually be worse than the punishment they were intended to replace (Adams et al, 1981; Evans, 1982).

'Back to justice' defines juvenile offending as a natural part of the process of the testing out of boundaries of acceptable behaviour that is commonplace in adolescence. It recognises that most adolescents who engage in offending behaviour grow out of crime as they make the transition into adulthood. It maintains therefore, that it is important not to over-react to that behaviour by imposing a 'criminal' label upon adolescents whilst they undergo the transitional process (Rutherford, 1992; Foster, 1989).

'New justice realism' and 'Punishment in the Community'

Just as the 1970s saw tensions in the juvenile justice system produced by two divergent ideologies, so the 1980s saw the increasing convergence of strategic thinking, albeit driven by differing motivation. The Thatcher government, elected largely on its commitment to 'law and order' and the apparently equal and opposite demands of reducing state intervention and public expenditure, needed to devise policies which satisfied both. This necessitated new approaches to punishment since the traditionally punitive option of incarceration was costly on the public purse. Reduction in the use of custodial sentencing became a common purpose therefore, to government and juvenile justice practitioners alike. The combination of these two forces led to the development of new provisions for juvenile offenders, which, during the 1980s, had the effect of significantly reducing the use of custodial sentencing.

In the latter half of the 1970s, as juvenile justice practitioners became aware of the increasing use of custody, a new organisation was formed - the National Intermediate Treatment Federation (NITFed) - as a forum in which practitioners could compare experiences and discuss ways of more appropriately targeting community resources towards those juveniles who were regarded as being 'at risk of custody'. Methods of working with young offenders were developed which directly challenged their offending behaviour as components within programmes which were specifically designed to be implemented as alternatives to custodial sentences. As such, this developing approach was practice-led, based on a desire to identify and promote sound working methods and to re-establish the credibility of social work in the court setting. From these origins in practice, theoretical contributions emerged which produced components of a correctional curriculum (see, for example, Denman, 1982).

In addition, theoretical work pioneered by the University of Lancaster (see, for example Giller, n.d.) began to address the issue of practitioner intervention in the operation of local juvenile justice systems in ways designed both to reduce the number of juvenile offenders processed through the courts as well as those receiving custodial sentences. The application of 'systems theory' and 'system management' became an increasingly important component of juvenile justice practice in the 1980s. From these origins a model of social work involvement in the juvenile justice system was developed - 'system intervention' - based on three interlocking features: maximum diversion, minimum intervention and system management.

'Maximum diversion' is a goal of juvenile justice practice. Diversion was originally devised on a 'welfare' model whereby the young person, rather than the offence, was the focus of concern (Davis, Boucherat and Watson, 1989) and was perceived in terms of pre-court consultations between the Police and Social Services Departments. In the 1980s the commitment to diversion has been sustained but the 'welfare' rationale has been replaced in favour of non-intervention and the concept extended to include all stages of the juvenile justice system. Thus the ultimate aim of 'maximum diversion' is to divert young people from crime, from prosecution and from custody.

One of the tools used in order to attain this goal is that of 'system management'. NACRO (1992) have described system management as:

> ... management - where possible - of the juvenile justice process as a single system with all agencies involved in working in co-operation (NACRO, 1992, p. 2).

The extent to which inter-agency co-operation has been achieved varies from one area to another. In some areas individual agencies have wished to retain their independence expressing the view that the justice system is best served by the adversarial process which leads to the balance of argument being heard in the court setting and, consequently, to open justice. This argument is based on the premise that enshrined in the role and responsibilities of each agency and department are the different and often competing tensions of the various sections of society. Each agency is said to reflect the differing interests of the law, victims of crime, defendants and the wider public interest. For example, Magistrates may argue that that it would be improper to engage in anything other than structural discussions with other parties to the justice system because to do so may run the risk of compromising their impartiality. Implicit in this argument is the assertion that those differing interests cannot be served through meaningful inter-agency co-operation and dialogue. In many areas of the country co-operation between agencies has led to a clarification of purpose and greater effectiveness in the juvenile justice process.

For Bell and Gibson (1991), system management is also a matter of intervention in the key stages of decision making within the juvenile justice process: influencing decisions at the point of arrest/charge, in juvenile liaison panels and bureaux, monitoring court reports and in court hearings.

In these key settings the purpose of intervention is to ensure the 'minimum intervention' in the lives of offenders (NACRO, 1992, p. 2) and in so doing, avoid the over-reaction to youthful offending mentioned by David Waddington (see above) and which features as a significant element of 'back to justice' (Rutherford, 1992; Foster, 1989).

At the juvenile liaison stage this entails facilitating greater use of cautioning rather than recourse to court proceedings. In those cases that are prosecuted court report monitoring is designed to bring about consistency in standards and to muster arguments in favour of the least intrusive sentence relative to the offence(s). At the post-sentencing stage 'minimum intervention' relies upon developing community programmes in which the courts can have confidence and which specifically address offending behaviour.

The provision of Specified Activity Orders were overtly encouraged in a Department of Health and Social Security circular in 1983 (DHSS Circular LAC 1983(3)) which announced financial support for voluntary organisations to establish projects. It also implied support for the 'system intervention' model through references to a commitment to reduce custodial sentencing, establish inter-agency bodies and bring about greater co-operation between existing agencies engaged in the juvenile justice system. However, as noted above, some of those schemes developed along the lines of a 'corporatist' approach.

Encouragement of the notion of diversion was also apparent in a circular issued by the Home Office in 1985 (HOC 14/1985, 'The Cautioning of Offenders') advocating cautioning as an alternative to court appearances. In the same year further support for cautioning juveniles came with the creation of the Crown Prosecution Service which rendered the prosecution of offenders independent of the Police. The Crown Prosecution Service's code of operation included the prosecution of juveniles only as a last resort in circumstances where there was a clear public interest to be served.

The Criminal Justice Act 1988 reinforced the status of the Specified Activity Order as a community alternative through the power given to courts to certify that the order was being imposed 'as a direct alternative to a custodial sentence' with the provision of imposing a custodial sentence in circumstances of breach. In addition, the 'custody criteria' introduced in 1982 were strengthened and Detention and Youth Custody Centre Orders were replaced by a single order of detention in a young offender institution.

The on-going convergence of 'system intervention' and social policy was also apparent in the provisions of the Children Act 1989 which, in addressing children's welfare needs, altered the status of remanded juveniles and placed a number of duties on local authorities in relation to young offenders as well as abolishing the s.7(&) Care Order. This Act placed a duty on local authorities to:

1. make arrangements for the prevention of crime by young people.

2. make arrangements for the diversion of young people from prosecution.

3. take steps to reduce the need for young people to be placed in secure accommodation, and

4. provide on-going advice, assistance and befriendment of young people on leaving local authority care or accommodation until their 21st birthday.

The combined effects of social policy and 'system intervention' in the 1980s was to reduce custodial sentencing by 81%, reduce the prosecution of juvenile by 70% and to reduce the number of known juvenile offenders by almost one-third between 1985 and 1990 (NACRO, 1992).

At the time this study was conducted in 1990 it was apparent that progress was being made. In the period immediately after completion of the research it appeared that changes brought about through the Criminal Justice Act 1991 would consolidate that progress to the benefit of young people and the community alike. However, in the last three years there has been a sudden and dramatic about-face in government policy towards juvenile offending. The policies that were seeming to have some impact have been abandoned in favour of a series of measures which appear to have been introduced because of their headline catching qualities more than their likely effectiveness in further reducing crime.

As I write, far from reducing the use of custody not only are the numbers of those incarcerated on the increase but the age of those whose liberty may be taken away is being reduced too. Far from looking to increase the age of criminal responsibility which has been a consistent theme since 1908, there are calls to lower the age at which children may be called to answer for their behaviour in a court of law. Stricter guidelines have been imposed in relation to the diversion of young offenders from court proceedings through Police cautioning. The combined effect of these measures is likely to bring more children and young people into the formal youth justice system; a process which has been shown to have a labelling effect leading to increased rather than decreased youth crime. The debate between competing ideologies has been replaced by an apparently cynical political dogma seemingly motivated by the need to bolster the popularity of the government; the short term gain of political survival being bought at the cost of the protection of the public and the needs and interests of young people.

Ideologies and 'race'

Although the convergence of ideology and social policy had led to reductions in both the use of custody and the prosecution of offenders, those reductions have not occurred consistently across the juvenile population. Black young people remain over-represented in many areas of the system and yet concepts of 'race' are absent as a consideration within any of the ideologies. Far from addressing the experience and place of Black young people in contemporary Britain ideology has, at best failed to recognise and address racism and, at worst, has entrapped Black people in stereotypical and mono-cultural responses.

The 'welfare' model, based as it is on notions of dysfunctional working class families has served to single out Black families since the definition of 'functioning' families is based on the values and norms of the dominant white culture. This has led to the effect of reinforcing 'blackness' as 'abnormal' and to the imposition of 'welfarist' measures. As a result Black children and young people have been particularly singled-out for inappropriate indeterminate sentencing, disproportionate to the seriousness of offending. Black children have been consistently over-represented in the care system. In relation to the 'justice' model, centred, as it is on notions of protection of the individual through the maintenance of rules of due process there has been a failure to acknowledge the scope for racism within the operation of the justice system.

'System intervention' arguably also compounds racism in the justice system. The recognition of the increased risk of custody in cases involving Black defendants appears to have had the effect of leading report authors to make alternative to custody recommendations in circumstances where they would not were the subject of the report white. The effect of this action is to reinforce a racist spiral. Since Black juveniles are regarded stereotypically as serious, persistent offenders an assumption may be made that the courts will be more inclined to consider a custodial sentence when faced with a Black defendant. This being so, report authors appear to be more inclined to recommend alternative to custody packages in cases involving Black defendants. However, by recommending alternative to custody packages in

44

these circumstances may have the unintended effect of transmitting the message to the court that the offences are indeed, so serious as to necessitate custodial alternatives and, paradoxically, have the effect of placing Black defendants at greater risk of a custodial sentence.

Parker et al (1989) showed how report authors were not at all accurate in anticipating the responses of courts to particular cases. This led to the imposition of alternative to custody sentences in cases where the court was originally contemplating a lesser sentence. Since the implementation of the Criminal Justice Act 1991 courts have been required when requesting Pre-sentence reports to give an indication of the sentence range that they are contemplating. In such circumstances, the risk of misinterpreting a court's intentions are much reduced. However, there remain a number of Black young people whose criminal careers have spanned this change in practice and who continue to be affected by the up-tariffing they have previously experienced.

It is upon these issues that this study is focused since it is only through the examination of the way the operation of the justice system impacts upon Black people that greater understanding will develop and lead to the emergence of new strategies which will address 'race' and the discrimination experienced by Black people.

The tariff system

Having considered how the juvenile justice system has developed and how the interplay between ideologies and social policy has been the framework within which both the courts and their administrative support mechanisms have functioned I turn in the second part of this chapter to the role of the tariff system within the process as it operated during the period of the study. I shall outline how sentences were arranged in a loose system assembled in ascending degrees of severity. I shall show how sentences which were imposed were frequently determined by considerations of an assessment of the seriousness of the current offence(s) and previous sentences that had been imposed. I shall go on to show that whilst there was some reluctance to acknowledge the existence of a tariff system there is evidence to demonstrate that courts operated a tariff of sentences. I shall demonstrate how the operation of a tariff system had implications for sentencing practice, how it impeded notions of individualized justice and how the operation of a tariff has impacted unequally upon Black defendants. Finally, I shall give some consideration to ideological issues associated with the operation of the tariff system.

The operation of a tariff of sentences

Over the course of years the general practice of the courts together with decisions made in the Court of Appeal have constructed a tariff of appropriate sentences for commonly occurring offence types. If sentencers impose a sentence above the appropriate point or range of points on the tariff it is likely to be reduced on appeal. In recent years it has also become possible for the Crown Prosecution Service to appeal against a sentence which was regarded as inappropriately low on the tariff. However, the tariff is not a prescriptive list of penalties to be followed in every circumstance. It operates by establishing ranges or brackets of disposals. If a sentence is imposed which is within the range indicated by the tariff it is unlikely to be reduced on appeal, even if it is at the uppermost level (Emmins, 1985).

It is regarded as axiomatic to the justice system that sentences imposed should be in proportion to the crime committed and the tariff is a measure by which sentencing may be judged. In addition to the practice of the courts the tariff is reinforced in a number of ways. the Magistrates' Association produce periodic guidelines to sentencing and sentencers also receive discreet guidance from the Chair and Deputy Chair of the local Magistrates' Bench. Furthermore, it is a function of the Stipendary Magistrate to indicate sentencing policy and advice is given too by the Clerk to the Justices (Emmins, 1985; Parker et al, 1989).

Evidence in support of a tariff of sentences is to be found in many studies (see, for example, Paley and Thorpe, 1980; Guest, 1980; Raynor, 1985; Tipler, 1986) and the concept of a tariff is common parlance amongst practitioners in the justice system. The essential premise is that offenders progress through the range of sentencing options with each successive court hearing, beginning with lower tariff options and moving ultimately towards custody at the top of the range.

A significant study was that conducted by the Home Office Research and Planning Unit which sought to answer the question 'Is there a tariff?' In this study, nine Petty Sessional Divisions (PSDs) were surveyed. It found that there was a clear top and bottom to the tariff but, between the two extremes, the relationship between sentences and key features of the cases were less obvious. In particular, the authors found a clear link between the sentence imposed and the criminal records of the offenders. However, the study showed a lack of consensus about the role of specific sentences. This was exemplified by the wide variation in the use of custodial sentences for apparently similar cases in different PSDs. Similarly, there was a significant difference noted in the sentencing patterns of different courts primarily with regard to the speed with which offenders progressed through the tariff (Moxon, Jones and Tarling, 1985).

It would appear then, that there are variations in the way the tariff is utilised and operated by different courts. This adds to the view that the tariff is a broad guide to generally accepted sentencing patterns. However, the evidence suggests that the tariff operates flexibly, such that it is not always possible in advance to predict the outcome of any particular case (Emmins, 1985). Emmins also notes that sentencing levels are dependant upon the interaction between, a) the gravity of the offence, b) the offender's previous criminal record and, c) their past experience, if any, of custody. Moxon et al (1985) found that the sentence imposed was largely determined by a combination of the seriousness of the offence together with previous disposals. However, although this study was published in 1985, it was based on data collected in 1978 which pre-dated the Criminal Justice Acts of 1982 and 1988 which impacted upon sentence criteria.

It is apparent from the more recent study conducted by Parker et al (1989) that the same factors, namely the seriousness of the offence and previous disposals were dominant factors, at least in the initial stages of sentence determination. In particular, they noted a reluctance on the part of Magistrates to deviate from the tariff when an offender had previously served a custodial sentence. However, this study went on to show how initial determinants became superseded by moral judgements based upon social background information which unintentionally fed prejudices (Parker et al, 1989, p. 51); a theme I shall return to later.

In their study of four PSDs (which included post-sentence interviews with Magistrates) Parker et al (1989) found considerable variation between the implementation of the tariff in different courts. The difficulty in predicting the likely outcome of each case was also noted. This had implications for accurately targeting community alternative packages. In a little over half the cases where a custodial sentence was imposed no alternative to custody recommendation was made. Conversely, they found a high proportion of alternative to custody recommendations in cases where Magistrates later revealed that the offenders were not deemed to be at risk of custody. This finding had particular implications for the study in relation to material contained in court reports and to the risk of 'up-tariffing' Black defendants.

The tariff cannot, therefore, be regarded as a precise mechanism. Different sentences are placed at different points in the system by different courts; even by Magistrates in the same court. This particularly relates to sentencing options in the middle range of the tariff. Whilst some courts may regard an Attendance Centre Order, for example, ranked alongside Community

47

Service Orders and Specified Activity Requirements, others use it as a mid-tariff option.

Variations are to be found, then, in the ranking of different disposals. Variations can also occur in the rate at which defendants progress through the tariff. Whilst some courts utilise the deterrent effect of each sentencing option in turn, others rapidly progress defendants through the various stages, often skipping a number of points. And so, although variations have been found in the operation of the tariff by different courts, nonetheless, there is evidence to support the principle that offenders graduate through the sentencing options with each successive court appearance according to a tariff of sentencing.

There are also arguments against the existence of a tariff. Mention has already been made of the lack of official recognition of such a concept. Moore (1985) argues that the tariff exists only in the minds of social workers and probation officers and goes on to express the view that this belief in a mythical concept does damage to notions of justice. One of the effects of this belief was to lead court report authors to attempt to 'out-guess' the courts by anticipating the likely outcome of any particular case. This in turn led to more severe sentencing. This concept of 'out-guessing' the courts was more significant in 1990, at the time of the study, especially in relation to the attempt to anticipate and compensate for racism at the sentencing stage.

Arguments against the existence of a tariff evidence the process by which Magistrates determine what sentence to impose. Axiomatic to sentencing practice is the notion of *mens rea*, that is, the guilty mind of the offender. However, courts are also required to take into account the welfare needs of the juvenile. Under-pinning the counter-balance of these two principles which guide sentencing is the regulatory impact of sentencing guidelines and the rulings of the Appeal Court. Moore (1985) argues, therefore, that instead of a tariff system courts operate according to a laid down sentencing process. Having identified the options available courts will amend their initial decision, normally in a downward direction, according to the mitigating circumstances of the case. These mitigating circumstances would include consideration of previous good character evidenced by the lack of a previous criminal record. In those cases where the defendant had a lengthy record, mitigation is more difficult to justify and would be reflected by less downward movement from the initial sentencing proposal. At the final stage in the process, the welfare needs of the juvenile would be taken into account and the decision adjusted accordingly.

The process which Moore (1985) outlines throws light on the findings of Parker et al (1989). This study found that initially sentence is determined through reference to the charges and access to the previous criminal record. That initial decision is modified having heard the submissions of the defence solicitor in mitigation and consideration of the court report contents. However, whilst the intention of those submissions may be to induce the Magistrates to impose a lesser sentence, because of the way in which the information is processed (see also, Brown, 1990) the effect may be to reinforce stereotypical constructs of the offender and, consequently, to less downward movement (if any) from the initially determined sentence.

Moore argues that were a tariff in operation courts would have very little flexibility: the sentence would be prescribed and it would not be possible to give consideration to other factors. This, he argues, would lead to even more anomalous sentencing practice. He cites the following example, a young person with previous custodial sentences appearing in court on this occasion charged with a more minor offence would, if the tariff were to apply, have a further custodial sentence imposed because the Magistrates would have no option but to impose a more stringent sentence than had been imposed previously.

It would appear that there are a number of flaws in this analysis. First, in relation to the example cited, many such examples of sentencing practice exist. Further custodial sentences are imposed on offenders charged with less serious offences following a custodial sentence (Parker et al, 1989). Secondly, the argument is based upon rigid notions of the tariff system which deny any other possibility of sentencing based upon downward movement on the tariff. Notions of tariff do not imply that progression is consistently in an upwards direction but rather that this is the general trend. Instead, there is some flexibility within the tariff system which is itself an imprecise concept; a trend visible in overview rather than universally discernible. Thirdly, Moore's argument discounts the different concepts of the tariff held by different PSDs such as were identified earlier. Nevertheless it does underline the principle that the more serious the offence, the less easy it is to justify departure from the tariff (Emmins, 1985).

Individualized sentencing

Sentences related to the gravity of the offence which are set within sentencing guidelines may be regarded as 'tariff sentences'. Those that reflect the individual and welfare needs of the offender may be regarded as 'individualized sentences' (Emmins, 1985). Individualized sentences are frequently those which involve less serious disposals and might include measures designed predominantly to address welfare needs.

From this basis it would be easy to assume that individualized sentences invariably lead to less severe sentencing. However, evidence suggests that on many occasions the opposite is true. For example, a 13 year old appearing in court for the first time charged with theft from a shop may be in a position whereby the offence is not regarded as serious in itself. However, further consideration of welfare need reveals parental neglect and may lead to the imposition of a supervision order on the grounds that advice and guidance is needed by the child. In these circumstances, the juvenile may be accelerated through the tariff system by an individualized sentence. The impact of that decision becomes apparent if the child re-offends having attained the age of 14 when, because a high-tariff disposal has previously imposed places the juvenile at risk of a custodial sentence.

In this context the 'up-tariffing' consequences of 'welfarist' intervention is observed and may be traced to the production of a court report. If a report had not been submitted revealing the 'home circumstances' the court may have been content to impose a fine or a discharge in response to the offence alone. Then, if social work concerns continued to exist about the issue of parental neglect the option remained open for that issue to be pursued separate to the criminal proceedings. It seems unjust that a child acquires a more punitive sentence as a means of gaining services she/he needs and yet the criminal courts have frequently been the referral point for children and young people who have been cause for concern by Police Officers and Magistrates. This is especially true at times of resource restraints when it is apparent that a child may not be prioritised unless a court order is in place.

Bottoms and Stelman (1988, p.19) cite a similar example wherein a supervision order is imposed on welfare grounds in a case involving a first time offender. In these circumstances should the juvenile re-offend Bottoms and Stelman suggest that the court may think that supervision has failed and consequently find it necessary to impose more stringent measures. Clearly it is important that welfare need is taken into consideration in sentencing. It is apparent that the original intention of considering the welfare needs of children art the point of sentence was that the identified need should mitigate against the full weight of the law being brought to bear not that the child should be further disadvantaged through more punitive sentencing. However, since this trend appears to be the product of responding to issues identified in court reports maybe in cases of first and second court appearances involving less serious matters agreements should be sought between youth justice agencies that court reports will not be routinely produced.

Rutherford (1992) points to the effect of 'system intervention' in diverting juveniles from court proceedings during the 1980s and early 1990s. He suggests that since many juveniles were dealt with outside the court setting the expectation might have been that those who did appear in court - serious and/or persistent offenders - would be subject to increasingly high tariff sentences. However, he notes that during this period sentencing trends have run generally in the opposite direction from that which might have been expected. As evidence for this view Rutherford points to the increased use of discharges and the decline in the use of custodial sentences. This would seem to suggest that a 'system intervention' approach had some success in diverting juveniles from crime through the principle and practice of minimum intervention.

In the course of this chapter I have traced the origins and development of the juvenile justice system and shown how ideologies have informed and been informed by social policy. I have demonstrated some of the tensions between the competing ideologies of 'welfare' and 'justice' and how the uneasy marriage of 'welfare' and 'justice' in the 1970s gave way to a convergent 'system intervention' path traced by practitioners and policymakers in the 1980s. I have identified that although ideology and social policy led to a reduction in court appearances and custodial sentences in the 1980s these reductions have not been experienced equally within all parts of the community and that over-representation of Black young people exists in all key stages of the system. It is this issue - disparity along racial lines - that now commands attention. Neither social policy not ideology have addressed the racist effects of the wider juvenile justice system and this issue continues to frame the agenda if justice is to be achieved for all parts of the community as we move into the new millennium.

Finally, I have pointed to the operation of the tariff system. I have suggested that despite the absence of official recognition a tariff of sentencing operates in the juvenile justice system. I have given examples of unintended consequences arising from the operation of the tariff and the ideological stance of practitioners. In the next chapter I shall examine a major social work tool in the justice system - the court report - and demonstrate how this too, has operated against the interests of Black people and has stereotypically framed 'race' in the context of dominant white cultural norms.

4   Social Inquiry Reports: Historical developments and literature review

In previous chapters, I have discussed the origins and nature of racism in Britain, traced the development of the juvenile justice system, addressed the issue of a sentencing tariff and considered ideologies. In the first part of this chapter, I shall trace the origins of Social Inquiry Reports (SIRs) and by reference to legislation, committee reports and government department circulars, show how they were established upon a model of juvenile justice which has never come into being. I shall further demonstrate that variations in standards of practice have arisen, in part, as a result of the practice of attempting to engender compassion amongst sentencers towards defendants. Finally, I shall consider the changes brought about by the transition from SIRs to Pre-sentence Reports (PSRs) and the introduction of national standards.

In the second part of this chapter I shall refer to existing literature and research to demonstrate concerns about standards of practice, particularly insofar as it reveals discriminatory practice in relation to Black defendants and young women. Wider issues of 'race' and the justice system are addressed in chapter 5. Finally in this chapter I shall examine a number of models of good court report practice.

The origins of SIRs

SIRs have their origins in the pleas made by Police Court Missionaries in the 1890s as they attempted to influence Magistrates into individualising sentencing according to the particular circumstances of the juveniles appearing before them. Enquiries into the background of offenders became more formalised in 1926 when Probation Rules were introduced, allowing for information to be presented concerning the social circumstances of any offender who might be suitable for a probation order.

Legislative authority to produce reports

Legislative authority to produce reports was introduced in the Children and Young Persons Act 1933. This was modified by the Departmental Committee on Social Services in Courts of Summary which recommended that the range of cases for which social investigation might take place should be broadened. The Criminal Justice Act 1948 allowed for the first time for report authors to make recommendations to the courts in relation to sentencing. In addition, courts were empowered to adjourn for reports to be prepared. This was a move which was intended to assist the court in determining the most suitable method of dealing with an offender by placing the offence and the offender into the context of their background and circumstances.

The framework for practice at the time of the study, 1990, was laid down in the Children and Young Persons Act 1969. Section 9 places a duty on local authorities to provide:

> ...the court, before which the proceedings are heard, with such information relating to home surroundings, school record, health and character of the person in respect to whom, the proceedings are brought, to appear to the authority, likely to assist the court.

The 1969 Act, as discussed earlier (see chapter 3), was a compromise following an earlier attempt to remove juveniles from the justice system. It was designed to decriminalise many types of cases, abolish punitive sentencing options and give the welfare needs of the juvenile paramountcy. It is clear that the intention of the Act was to provide the courts with social background information, through SIRs, as a means of identifying areas of need; a diagnosis of the aspects of the juvenile's lifestyle that required treatment.

Social background information in the context of justice

As a result of the partial implementation of the 1969 Act, the juvenile justice system operated from the 1970s on the basis of a dual philosophy. The original notion of punishment in proportion to crimes committed as a result of deliberate choice remained but was overlaid with a philosophy of treating the victims of social inequality and deprivation who, symptomatically, committed offences. The effect of this was to produce two separate agendas; one for those who provided social background information (SIR authors) and the other for those who were responsible for determining sentence based upon social background information (the sentencers).

The parameters of SIR content indicated in the 1969 Act had their origins in the Streatfield Report (HMSO, 1961) which recommended that SIRs should contain information about the offender's personality, character and background. It should also portray her/his present environment and surroundings, together with details of the offenders work record and attitude to work, prospects of employment, attitude to the offence(s) and the stated reason for offending. In the context of juvenile offenders, work records and attitudes were to be replaced by school reports.

With certain modifications indicated by government department circulars, the principles of the Streatfield Report remained in force as the predominant SIR guidelines. Subsequently, requirements were issued for other matters to be addressed in SIRs including the expression of opinions by SIR authors concerning the likely response of the offender to particular disposals (Home Office, 1971a, 1971b) and specific sentence recommendations, including the optimum length of order (Home Office, 1974). As a result SIR preparation continued to be based on guidelines intended for a juvenile justice system operating on a different philosophy than actually prevailed in the courts.

Removal of local authority discretion

The Children and Young Persons Act 1969 had placed a duty on local authorities to produce SIRs in those circumstances where it was felt that it would assist the court. The content of reports remained at their discretion. However, the Criminal Justice Act 1982, s.2 placed the obligation on courts 'in every case, to obtain a social inquiry report, unless it considers it unnecessary to be furnished with one'.

Theoretically, this added significance to SIRs, as did the requirement, stated in the 1982 Act, that in furtherance of the intention to diminish the use of custodial penalties, report authors should give consideration to appropriate community alternative options (s.2). Furthermore, the Act nominated SIRs as a key piece of evidence in any subsequent appeal against sentence. However, these modifications did not address the issues of practice and content and SIRs continued to be produced according to the principles established by the Streatfield Report highlighting areas of individual and family inadequacy, dysfunction and need.

Concerns that existed about SIRs at an official level were less to do with the framework of social background information but instead focused on the length of reports, the relevance of certain information and the objectivity of authors (Home Office, 1983a). Home Office Circular 17/1983 sought to encourage authors to be concise and selective about the contents and, where possible, to show that information gained from defendants had been verified elsewhere. In the same year, Circular 18/1983 laid down guidelines defining the purpose of recommendations as assisting the court in determining the best way to deal with an offender and offering an informed assessment of the likely consequences of a particular sentencing option.

These circulars reflected the on-going ambivalence towards SIRs. Authors continued to provide detailed personal histories, hoping to engender compassion on the part of the court towards the defendant. The courts, however, were being overwhelmed by the length of reports and wished them to be shorter but without losing the quantity or quality of information provided about the offender (Brown, 1991).

Reference to 'race' and culture emerged for the first time in 1986 (Home Office, 1986). In a circular primarily directed at the function of SIRs in the adult courts, stress was placed on the need to bring out significant aspects of social background where 'race' and culture featured as an issue. However, the guidance was limited to a simple observation that issues of 'race' and culture should be addressed in SIRs where such factors threw light upon the subject's offending. Nevertheless, it is clear that through legislation and the publication of guidelines, attempts were being made to enhance the status of the SIR as an influential document in court proceedings. However, they continued to be produced in a climate of differing objectives on the part of authors and the courts and without genuine concern about the effects of reports for Black defendants.

Potential influence and concerns about practice

De la Motta described SIRs as 'possibly the most significant document to be presented before the court' (1984, p. 28). Yet that significance would appear to have been doubted by SIR authors who questioned the extent to which reports were read or the level of influence they had on sentencing outcomes Parker et al, 1989; Brown, 1991). Similarly it appears that even when the extent of influence was accepted there was uncertainty as to which components had influence. Consequently, there was uncertainty about what information to include and what to leave out. As Raynor noted:

Despite the production of tens and thousands of reports on juveniles every year and the publication of a good deal of research, this remains an area of practice in which it is difficult to discern consistent policies and standards, or even, a common understanding of aims (1985a, p. 25).

The confusion that arose produced a considerable variation in reporting techniques and standards which was of much concern. Indeed, there was real doubt as to whether the interests of offenders were being safeguarded in a considerable number of the reports that were written. Such was the level of concern that after many years of SIR production, legislation enacted, policy guidelines published and research findings utilised to assess the quality of reports, the National Association for the Care and Resettlement of Offenders (NACRO) were moved to appeal to local authorities to:

> Ensure that SIR writers are clear about the purpose of the report and include only relevant, unambiguous and non-judgmental information about the offence and the young person's offending behaviour (NACRO, 1988, p. 1).

The reasons for the lack of clear understanding about the purpose and content of SIRs was to be found in their ambivalent origins and the evolutionary process they had undergone which was influenced by changing ideology and political thinking. Uncertain SIR practice developed in the shifting sands of juvenile justice philosophy. Having considered these origins, I now turn to practice issues and examine the observations that have been made about the standard of reports.

SIR practice: research studies

A good deal of research was published about SIR practice from a variety of sources (for a summary see Raynor, 1985a). Many individuals, pressure groups and agencies sought to offer clarification about SIR practice. Each addressed the issue from the perspective of their own place in the juvenile justice system. The Home Office sponsored a large amount of work in this area in an attempt to examine standards and identify principles for good practice. Local authorities and the probation service produced guidelines for staff reflecting local policy. Individual researchers studied SIR practice together with practitioner groups such as NACRO, the Association for Juvenile Justice (AJJ) and NITFed with the intention of improving practice for the benefit of defendants and for the purpose of devising strategies for influencing courts away from custodial measures. As a result, there was a body of material relating to SIR practice emanating from a variety of sources. However, because there was no unified voice the overall effect of the advice that was given to authors was confusing (Waters, 1991).

An early study was that conducted by Perry (1974) who, in a comprehensive programme of research, found wide variation in standards of SIR practice. This study considered the whole process of report preparation from the point of allocation to the presentation of the completed report. Perry found, in a sample of 253 SIRs studied and authors interviewed, that there was a wide range of deficient practice. Authors were frequently unaware of the precise nature of the charges to be faced by defendants and were often uninformed about their previous criminal record. Investigations were generally limited to one interview with the defendant and, occasionally, one parent (cf. the current National Standard for PSRs). Little attempt was made to corroborate information that was given. Perry also found that there was a risk of collusion between authors and defendants in that each of them had issues that they wanted to feature in the interview but neither of them allowed the discussion to go beyond the predetermined issues. Similarly, he found that there was considerable, misplaced trust in previous assessments and reports, whether initiated by the same or another report author. Interviews in the defendant's home occurred infrequently and so too did consultation with any other agency involved in the case.

With regard to report contents, Perry found significant variation in length, content and quality and that many areas of investigation were overlooked. Recommendations were not always made. In those cases where they were, recommendations rarely flowed logically from the body of the report. On occasions they were tentative and apparently made on the basis of the author attempting to 'second-guess' what the court might have imposed anyway.

Thorpe's study (1979) focused upon report contents, the variation in the use of reports and the correlation between reports and sentencing outcomes. One of the main findings related to the apparent vacuum in which authors felt they wrote reports. Authors were uncertain about what information courts needed to determine the appropriate sentence. In the absence of such information authors themselves determined what they should include, often on a case by case basis. In consequence, there was considerable variation found in relation to the length of reports, the format used and the contents. Nevertheless, Thorpe found that reports influenced sentencing, especially when a clear recommendation was made. However, he found no correlation between the length of the report and the sentencing outcome.

As a result of his findings, Thorpe proposed that SIRs should be shortened; leaving out that information which the courts would ordinarily obtain from other, perhaps, better informed sources, eg, details of the defendants previous criminal record. In addition, he proposed that SIRs should not be prepared for first time offenders on the basis that offences were rarely serious enough to warrant anything other than a non-custodial sentence. This removed the possibility of the defendant being moved up-tariff on the grounds of welfare considerations.

Both Perry and Thorpe advocated closer working relationships between authors and Magistrates and proposed that mechanisms should be put into place to allow for feedback and discussion. However, whilst there would appear to be some benefit to be gained by closer working relationships, Magistrates and authors have different tasks to perform within the system. For example, it is not the function of report authors to take account of *all* the factors which the court must have regard to. At the same time, there are power issues at work in the operation of the justice system. Magistrates command authority and respect. Consequently, they may be seen to define what is and what is not good practice. However, there are matters of professional independence which requires social work to define its own standards of practice commensurate with its function and purpose within the justice system. It is important for the interests of defendants that social work does not succumb to pressure to have practice issues defined by Magistrates. It is particularly important that social workers do not strive to adopt principles determined by the Magistracy in the name of maintaining their credibility.

A standardised format for SIRs?

In view of the perceived shortcomings of investigations and SIR preparation a proposal was made to standardise the report format as a means of overcoming poor practice. Perry (1974) suggested that to do so would lead to more effective investigation by prescribing the issues that should be explored. The Morrison Report (1962) however, took the view that the standardisation of reports would not serve the best interests of offenders, even though it was recognised that lack of standardisation resulted in variations in practice.

Standardisation was deemed to contain other risks which mitigated against the desired improvement in practice. Since both the report author and the defendants are individuals, it would be inappropriate to impose a rigid format that may impinge on the effectiveness of author in conveying information to the court. Standardisation, it was suggested, might not lead to improvement in practice. Instead, it was argued that practice would be improved by increasing awareness, knowledge and skills through training. Ultimately standardisation of court reports has come into effect with PSRs. It is interesting to note that in many cases the standards have been set at a point lower than was regarded to be good SIR practice and that the definition of content has not been universally applauded by Magistrates.

Supervision orders and SIRs

One of the originally intended functions of SIRs was to make observations about the anticipated response of the defendant to a probation order. In circumstances where supervision orders feature as the recommendation of SIRs, there was an expectation that the report included information highlighting:

1. The reason why a supervision order was seen by the author to be appropriate.

2. The issues to be addressed through the supervision order.

3. The likely response of the defendant to a supervision (Harris and Webb, 1987).

Harris and Webb's study (1987) examined several areas of the relationship between supervisor and client. When examining SIRs, they found that packages of supervision were rarely outlined in the reports. Neither were reasons given why supervision was considered to be appropriate as a sentencing option.

Reynolds (1982) undertook a study of SIRs prepared in connection with juveniles on supervision orders. She compared reports written leading up to the imposition of the supervision order and compared them with reports prepared for previous and subsequent court appearances. She found that those used at the time supervision orders were imposed were similar in content to those that had previously been prepared arguing for lesser disposals. There were few cases where specific account was taken of the recommendation of a supervision order. Where reasoned, logical argument was made in the report for further welfarist intervention following the imposition of the supervision order, Magistrates were inclined to adopt the recommendation. Where no such argument or recommendation was made, more punitive measures were imposed.

Ball's (1984) study of SIRs found serious shortcomings in authors' knowledge of their clients as portrayed in reports. Furthermore, he found that it was often difficult to distinguish between information about the defendant and the authors professional assessment of them.

SIR recommendations and sentencing

Many studies focused upon the extent to which Magistrates adopted recommendations contained in SIRs (see, for example, Perry, 1974; Thorpe, 1979; Ball, 1984; Tipler, 1985). Considerable variation was found in the rate of uptake of recommendations. Whilst some studies reported adoption rates of 75%-80% (Perry, 1974; Thorpe, 1979; Ball, 1984), Tipler (1985) found a rate of 27%-35%. Caution needs to be exercised in relation to up-take levels since the adoption of a recommendation does not necessarily demonstrate that Magistrates have been influenced into imposing some other sentence than they would otherwise have done. Reference has already been made to the practice of report authors 'second-guessing' the intentions of Magistrates. Such correlation that exists may reflect the success of authors' anticipation skills.

Many social work and probation service agencies adopted a policy of not recommending custodial sentences. These decisions were based on the basis that custodial sentences are purely punitive in nature; that they offer little opportunity to address the issues and behaviour that led to offending and also, that they require the defendant to be detained in institutions, often with other, more sophisticated offenders, where an offending lifestyle is the norm.

As mentioned earlier, the Criminal Justice Act 1982 directed SIR authors to identify appropriate community alternative options where it was perceived that there was a high risk of custody. It would appear, however, that in practice, reports often did not address custody. Neither did they always include information relating to appropriate community alternative provisions, perhaps reflecting the perceptions of the authors that in those cases non-custodial recommendations were unlikely to be adopted. The absence of information about alternative to custody provisions were also reinforced on occasion by the absence of any recommendation or, in some cases, a direct or indirect custodial recommendation (Parker et al, 1989).

It is apparent that Magistrates interpreted the absence of recommendation as an implicit recommendation of a custodial sentence (Parker et al, 1989,

Brown, 1991). It is apparent also, that in an attempt to accommodate the competing demands of court and employer, authors used indirect references to custody. For example, a report might contain an observation to the effect that the author is 'unable to assist the court' with a recommendation, or, more explicitly, that the offender needs to be directed towards a 'structured regime in order to instil discipline'. In these circumstances, not only does a failure to discuss community alternative options represent a failure to comply with the requirements of the Criminal Justice Act 1982, it also fails to represent the interests of the offender. Instead, it seems more likely that these practices were driven by the perceived need of the social work and probation services to protect or enhance their credibility with the courts.

SIRs and objectivity

Emmins (1985) noted that reports often lacked objectivity and on occasion were framed in an unsatisfactory way. He found that the 'general tenor of the ... officer's report may be just as damning as a recommendation for custody' (p. 69).

Similarly, Parker et al (1989) found evidence of reports written in a subjective and emotive manner, to the point that they engaged in character assassination. There was also evidence in the study of reports being motivated by revenge on the part of the author in response to a perceived lack of co-operation or act of incivility on the part of the defendant. In these circumstances it may be anticipated that a negative message will be communicated to sentencers. The origins of that negative message, however, are unlikely to be clear. Consequently, Magistrates will be left with a view of the defendant which may not be representative of her/his circumstances. Nevertheless, it is on this basis that sentence will be imposed. The outcome is that the defendant was effectively sentenced for their behaviour towards the report author rather than the offence that was committed.

Report authors are required to make judgements about defendants. It is apparent then, that authors do not operate in a value-vacuum. Social work is not value-free but value-laden. Social workers bring to their work their own values and those of their employers as well as the social work profession and the community. These values are influenced by those of the people, professions and agencies around which authors live and work. It is important therefore, that social workers are aware of their own value base and acknowledge the range and diversity of other values represented by people and institutions within the community as a whole. Equally, it is important that authors are aware of their own prejudices and devise concious strategies to overcome them before they become embodied as part of the report.

Each individual carries with them some notion of what lifestyles constitute normality. The shape of this model of normality evolves over time and through experience. When we observe other people, what becomes most noticeable is that behaviour and lifestyle which deviates from our model of 'normality'. When observing people who have had similar life experiences the extent of their deviation from our model of 'normality' may be relatively small. As those life experiences become increasingly different so the deviation from our model increases. Therefore, differences of class, culture, ethnicity, gender, religion, etc. become more apparent to us. It is these features which then can easily be translated into the report and become sources for potential discrimination.

The studies noted above did not attempt to identify potential sources of discrimination. Other studies that have included 'race' and/or gender dimensions have revealed widespread bad practice which has had the effect of seriously disadvantaging Black and/or female defendants. Bean (1971) noted:

> Traditionally, arguments about disparities in sentencing, have hitherto, been directed at the decision maker, those writing reports were excluded. The nature of the evidence presented, so far, suggests that probation officers also, contribute to these disparities (p. 174).

SIRs and 'race'

Court report content analysis studies relating to Black defendants have found widespread discriminatory practice. This practice has ranged from apparently inadvertent cultural insensitivity to overt racism. Material that would have been regarded as irrelevant in relation to white defendants has been included and given prominence in reports about Black defendants. A frequently witnessed occurrence relates to the inclusion of information about the migration and religious practices of Black people. This practice serves to negate Black people's contribution to the community and denies their right to live in Britain (Dominelli, 1988, p. 118).

There is also evidence of an underlying trend not to acknowledge the power and authority implicit in the social work function. Social work contains a powerful social control function. It is steeped in the values of the dominant culture (Chiquada, 1989). Indeed, Dominelli (1988) makes the point more specifically and argues that social work, as a framework of thinking, is steeped in white, middle-class attitudes. In this context, as noted above, it is apparent that report authors carry with them norms based on their own culture and fashioned by professional training. In preparing a court report, authors compare and contrast both their perceptions of the defendant and their understanding of the racial and cultural context of the defendant's background against the author's own model of 'normality'. Depending on the level of cultural awareness and sensitivity, this process may be influenced, to a greater or lesser degree, by stereotypes. The assessment that is made, therefore, may reflect the perceptional base of the author as much as it portrays the characteristics and background of the defendant. Overall objectivity in report writing, therefore, is a difficult ideal to achieve. Dominelli (1988) makes the point very powerfully. In social work:

'White social workers' concerns to get clients behaving appropriately, has problematised ethnicity by judging Black people, according to dominant stereotypes of their ethnic grouping (p. 123).

It has been noted that SIRs were predominantly constructed on a 'welfare' model, which has its roots in the process of decriminalising offending behaviour. This entails identifying areas of dysfunction and proposing corrective treatment which, in turn, leads the author to search for negative characteristics and problems within families, as indicators of the locus of responsibility for offending behaviour (Whitehouse, 1986). It is not difficult, therefore, to see the link between disadvantage in the power relationship between the SIR author and the Black subject and how that power relationship is communicated to the court. It is against this back-drop that content analysis of SIRs written in relation to Black defendants has been undertaken and has produced alarming findings. There is a tendency not to accept Black people as British (Whitehouse, 1986). Furthermore, Blackness is defined as problematic by white social workers (Dominelli, 1988).

Comparative content analysis studies

In a comparative study of SIRs written in relation to Black and white defendants in Leeds, Pinder (1984) matched reports based on age, gender, previous convictions and current charge(s). He found that there was a different pattern to the relationship between recommendations and sentences regarding Black defendants in comparison with whites. When looking at SIR content, he found discrepancies in each of three areas studied. First, there was an absence of a coherent and explicit framework for presenting Black British identity in the reports. Secondly, there was an absence of an individual, pathological ideology from the accounts of Black British defendants when compared with whites. Thirdly, there was an absence of excuses for the behaviour of Black British defendants compared with whites. Overall, Pinder noted an assumption that a white person is British but a Black person is Black.

Two court based studies; one in Birmingham, the other in Hackney, identified further examples of disadvantage experienced by Black defendants, which had consequences for them in terms of relative sentencing. Pimm and Lines (1987) studied 225 reports presented in all Birmingham courts between 10-21 March, 1986. References to defendants' racial origins were made twice as often in reports about Black defendants than those about whites. In addition, analysis revealed cases which linked offending to 'race' and blamed victims for racist attacks. In a content analysis study based on reports being read by pairs of analysts, reports on Black people were regarded as more negative. It was noted too, that there was a failure to recognise cultural diversity and increased reference to family disunity and mental health problems amongst Black defendants. With regard to unemployment and social deprivation, there was a tendency to regard this as a problem arising from individual inadequacy where the subject was Black.

As mentioned above, reports were read by pairs of analysts, in the first place, independently of each other. All analysts were probation officers and, consequently, were privy to the same agenda and framework for report presentation as the authors. Observations were recorded on a checklist comprising eight headings related to potential areas of discriminatory practice, e.g. stereotyping, value judgements, white culture as norm, etc. Thus the analysts were led by the way the checklist was formulated to observe particular facets. The checklist also contained a cross-tabulation on which discriminatory practice, as defined by the authors of the study, was recorded, together with, relevance of the material to the case, whether it was harmful to the individual and whether it reinforced existing prejudice. On the basis that the reports were analysed by probation officers, steeped in the same professional culture, there was scope for the same subjectivity as that of the report authors. If the reports had been analysed by people other than probation officers, say, for example, Magistrates, Judges or clients - receivers of the material rather than transmitters - the analysis may have produced different findings.

In terms of recommendations, Pimm and Lines found that 51% were adopted for white defendants, compared with 39% for Blacks. There are difficulties in drawing too many conclusions from these findings in relation to recommendation adoption because too many questions remain unanswered. Were the recommendations proportionate to the seriousness of the offences? Were there any differences in the level at which recommendations were pitched for Black and white defendants? Were the sentences imposed more or less punitive than the recommendations?

Where no recommendation was made, all cases involving Black defendants resulted in custodial sentences, whilst 43% of whites received community alternative sentences. This was in spite of the fact that white defendants faced more serious charges. Again, the imponderable here, is whether this finding reflects more on report authors judgements or sentencers decision making.

The reports studied were presented to all courts in Birmingham; juvenile, magistrates and Crown courts. As a result, the cases involved would include a proportion of serious offences, including, perhaps, those for which custodial sentences are proscribed. In these circumstances, the low levels of recommendations being adopted may be explained by report authors adhering to agency policy not to recommend custody. However, it is apparent that recommendations made in relation to Black defendants, however well argued, would be less likely to be effective when set against the negative report contents indicated above.

In Hackney, Tipler (1989) found similar evidence of disadvantage to Black defendants arising from discriminatory practice in SIRs presented in the juvenile court. In particular, he noted that SIRs were a source of disadvantage in two ways. First, reports relating to Black juveniles tended to contain higher-tariff recommendations than for whites. Secondly, there was a greater likelihood of no recommendation being contained in reports relating to Black juveniles than whites. This also resulted in higher tariff sentencing for Black juveniles.

Previous disposals and recommendations

From this study, Tipler noted a potential cycle of disadvantage arising from the practice of authors using the previous disposal as the basis for making recommendations in SIRs. He found that it was common practice for authors to note the previous disposal imposed on a defendant and, in the current SIR, to recommend the next highest sentence on the tariff. In these circumstances, if the recommendation was not adopted and a higher tariff disposal was imposed, the result was that the baseline for future reports was higher still. Furthermore, he found that this scenario impacted most on Black juveniles. Tipler cited the following example:

> Two young men, one white and one Black, appear separately in a juvenile court on a charge of theft. For both it is their first offence and neither has been cautioned. Their offences are similar. For this first offence, the Magistrates have in mind one of the two lowest sentencing options available, either a conditional discharge or a more severe fine. The white young man receives a conditional discharge, while the Black young man is fined.
>
> Subsequently, they both appear in court again, also separately, on the more serious charge of burglary. This time a Social Enquiry Report is requested in both cases. The social workers in the cases draw up their reports, and in both cases, decide that the case is sufficiently serious that the recommendations must be at a higher level. The benchmark that the social workers use in these cases is different. In the case of the white young man, taking him up the scale of sentencing will result in the recommendation of a fine. In the second case, the recommendation will be supervision (1989, p. vi).

Tipler concludes that the method of determining the recommendation in both cases was entirely equal. However, by ignoring the inequalities inherent in the juvenile justice process, it had the effect of placing the Black defendant at a significantly higher level in the tariff. The consequences of re-offending would, in these circumstances, be very different for each of them. Re-offending after a fine being imposed, for the white defendant, might lead to the imposition of a supervision order, whereas re-offending whilst on a supervision order might result in a custodial sentence being imposed on the Black defendant.

The example Tipler cites graphically highlights the dangers inherent in using previous disposals as the baseline for future recommendations, particularly for Black defendants. It exposes deficiencies in giving primacy to previous disposals (see chapter 3) which, by definition, diminishes the importance of individual circumstances and the impact of the justice system on Black people.

There are problems with Tipler's example, however. As noted previously, the tariff is not an exact science. There are variations in its application within and between courts. Nevertheless, it is not unusual for fines and conditional discharges to be ranked similarly on the tariff and used as mutual alternatives. However, dependant upon the length of the conditional discharge and the timing of the new offence, in the example, the white defendant might additionally face the breach of the discharge as well as the burglary and might, consequently, be at a greater risk of a high tariff disposal. Nevertheless, the principle remains and the prospect of disparity exists and, given the foregoing evidence about SIR content and Black juveniles, the risk of disparity of sentencing is compounded.

The positive use of cultural factors

In the light of this evidence it was frequently thought to be appropriate to amplify the positive aspects of the defendants cultural experiences in SIRs. However, Taylor (1981) pointed out a potential pitfall with this practice. She suggested that it is not a helpful practice as it was unlikely that the reader would have any conception of the lifestyle or tradition to which it related. Indeed, in the light of the findings of Parker et al (1989) and Brown (1990) which showed how social background information was used to reinforce stereotypical and prejudicial moral constructs which were used against defendants in sentencing, even the most positively motivated inclusion of cultural experiences were likely to disadvantage Black defendants. Nevertheless, Taylor (1981) argued that whilst cultural factors do not excuse crime, an explanation of the cultural context may produce some understanding of the motivation behind certain acts.

This placed SIR authors in something of a dilemma. Anti-racist practice demands that social workers should not disadvantage Black defendants. In such circumstances SIR authors may have felt inclined to contextualise Black defendants within a racist environment and seek to engender compassion for the circumstances in which they were placed and in which the offence has been committed. However, as noted above, to do so placed the author at risk of providing information which, instead of mitigating on behalf of the defendant, may be used prejudicially against her/him. In these circumstances, the report author runs the risk of failing to wholly represent the subject by omitting to address pertinent issues but, at the same time risks disadvantaging the subject if issues are addressed since, whilst the author may be in control of the material that is included, s/he is not in control of how that material is received, interpreted and used.

Whilst it is appropriate in court reports to place the offence in context, including the cultural dimension, in the specific case of the individual defendant, court reports are not the forum through which to educate Magistrates and raise 'race' awareness. The process of mutual education of

67

partnership agencies in the justice system must take place away from the court room where the liberty of any individual is not at risk.

Models of good practice

So far, much has been said of bad SIR practice and that which ought to be avoided. I turn now to frameworks that were presented as models for good practice. In terms of the overall tenor of SIRs, Bean (1976) is unequivocal. 'SIRs should be avowedly diagnostic, and the recommendation attempt to make the punishment fit the offender' (p. 183). Raynor (1985a), however, took a different view:

> Traditionally, they [SIRs] have been seen as the provision of expert advice about the most appropriate sentence: that is, the sentence most likely to be effective in reducing the offender's tendency to re-offend. Thus they fit well into a 'treatment', or 'rehabilitational' model of sentencing, based on the idea that given enough information about the history, personality and social situation of an offender, it should be possible to devise a scientifically appropriate sentence, which will have a rehabilitative effect (p. 25).

This is an optimistic view which research offers little to support. Despite the production of more and longer SIRs, recidivism persisted. Studies that have been undertaken, some of which have been referred to above, whilst pointing out bad practice, have often produced conflicting guidelines for good practice. This in part reflects the lack of ideological clarity and singleness of purpose in the justice system. But even the pragmatists could not agree.

Powell (1985), writing from her position in a court office, stated 'report writing is about getting results, and getting results, involves the use of strategies' (p. 91). That is to say, the effective use of SIRs had more to do with using them tactically than it had to do with faithfully portraying individual defendants through the production of life histories. Reynolds (1982) also indicated the need to develop courtroom strategies, particularly in order to avoid the use of custody.

Hazell (1987) produced a six point plan for effective SIR preparation:

1. The withdrawal of the automatic preparation of SIRs on first and, in certain circumstances, second court appearances.

2. SIRs should contain recommendations for credible sentencing options.

3. They should operate on the principle of the minimal level of intervention, or the least detrimental alternative.

4. They should be compatible with the agency's objectives in relation to changes in sentencing options.

5. There should be an awareness of the objectives of other agencies/actors in the juvenile justice system, e.g. Crown Prosecution Service, Magistrates, etc.

6. There should be recognition of the crucial importance of a) quality control, b) monitoring and, c) gate-keeping (pp. 1-2).

These principles, like those offered by other writers, make firm proposals in relation to the strategic use of SIRs based on principles of 'system intervention' but add little to the debate about content and say nothing about the issue of 'race'. Reference is made to notions of 'quality control', 'monitoring' and 'gate-keeping' but with no indication of what represents quality or good practice. Without such guidelines these mechanisms have no benchmark to uphold.

Ball (1984) and Tipler (1985) argued that unrestricted SIR production increases the use of custody. Ball's study of practice in Manchester led to claims that the implementation of a joint social services and probation service policy not to produce reports in cases of first appearances had considerable impact on the reduction of committals to Crown Court with recommendations for Borstal Training. Tipler also found that in cases where no report was provided, lower tariff sentences were imposed. The inference from these findings was that there was something about SIR content which increased the risk of higher tariff sentencing. Parker et al (1989) and Brown (1991) have shown how social background information led to capricious moral judgements which affected sentencing. Consequently, they argued that defendants appearing in court for the first time should not be placed at greater risk of a more intrusive sentence than if a report had not been produced.

Quality control mechanisms were widely advocated based on a number of different models. Tipler (1985) and Walker (1985) both argued for team or peer group discussion of reports. Whitehouse (1986) suggested that authors should also check their perceptions with clients and invite them to make their own observations.

It has been noted however, that the messages transmitted within reports are not necessarily those that are received, neither is the interpretation placed on the contents that which was intended. In this context it is important to gain some understanding of the way in which reports are received by those who read them and who base sentencing decisions on them.

Mair (1985) found that whilst reports were generally received favourably by Magistrates this was because of the factual information rather than the sentencing recommendations made. This reinforces the view that the material content could be used to substantiate different conclusions from those that were intended. If the outcome was that information contained in the report confirmed Magistrates first impressions of the defendant and contributed to the imposition of prejudicial sentencing, it should not be surprising that reports were received favourably by Magistrates. The question arises, however, of how to distinguish between the information Magistrates *needed* in order to determine the sentence from what they *wanted*, which may simply have reinforced their own subjectivity.

Where there was evidence of good practice and of the recommendation flowing logically from the body of the report, it might have been expected that Magistrates, in receiving the report favourably, would also receive the recommendation favourably. However, it has been seen that often recommendations did not flow in this way and frequently, were not well argued. It is also apparent that social workers have assumed that information contained in reports would be received in the same manner in which it was intended. Clearly, the evidence is that this is not necessarily the case.

It has been noted how Magistrates 'construct' an impression of the defendant's character based upon a moral assessment. Parker et al (1989) found that information in SIRs was treated cautiously, if not with suspicion, on the premise that social workers were 'on the side of the defendant' and, consequently, were less than objective in their portrayal of the circumstances. Magistrates, then, dismissed the impartiality of reports and rejected recommendations accordingly. Parker et al (1989) revealed that Magistrates also sifted reports in search of material which supported their own 'construct' of the defendant, thus confirming stereotypical prejudices. These findings, together with Brown's (1991) are significant since they give insight into the process of receiving, interpreting and validating information prior to sentencing. The observation that is made of a lack of social work impartiality legitimises Magistrates' dismissal of the report content and recommendation and allows for selective re-interpretation of the content to confirm impressions and stereotypes. These findings have clear impact on the considerations social workers need to make when deciding what information should be included in court reports and what should be excluded as being likely to prejudice the sentencing outcome. It has been argued that since the introduction of PSRs and 'gate-keeping panels' that reports are more objective and less discriminatory. However, at this stage, there is no evidence to support this view and until it is known to the contrary PSRs must be presumed to carry the same risks.

Addressing custody in SIRs

Having recognised how moral judgements are used prejudicially by Magistrates against defendants and the increased risk of custody that results, it becomes important to address the issue of the consideration of custodial sentencing within reports. West Midlands Intermediate Treatment Association (WMITA, 1984) produced guidelines for good practice which included emphasis on the criteria that must be satisfied before a custodial sentence may be imposed. They suggested that in cases where there is deemed to be a risk of custody SIRs should directly address those criteria, making clear those areas where SIR authors believed the criteria were not met and spelling out the detrimental impact of custody in principle as well as in relation to the specific circumstances of the defendant.

In order to do this authors needed to be able to accurately identify those cases where there was a real risk of custody. Parker et al (1989) noted that there was considerable variation between the perceptions of SIR authors and Magistrates concerning which defendants were at risk of a custodial sentence. In certain cases it was noted that defendants were perceived to be 'destined for custody' by Magistrates and that no other disposal was appropriate. In these circumstances a recommendation for anything but custody was rejected. However, a number of other cases were identified in which the issue of custody was 'open to negotiation'. It was in these cases that SIRs could have the greatest influence through addressing the custody criteria and promoting well defined community alternatives. The crucial factor was the accurate identification of those cases which were 'destined for custody' and those which were 'open to negotiation'. Studies have repeatedly shown that SIR authors could not accurately identify the cases of greatest risk and, consequently SIR content was not appropriately targeted.

71

Some observations on good practice

It has been shown that SIRs were framed by a 'welfarist' intention to decriminalise offending behaviour but that this intention was never adopted, largely because of the failure to carry the principles through to legislation. In these circumstances, diagnostic SIRs, highlighting inadequacy and dysfunction and recommending disposals on the basis of treating individual pathology, did not serve the interests of juvenile offenders. Dislocated catalogues of pathologies have often served to validate more intrusive intervention rather than engendering compassion for the offender. References in reports to 'broken homes', 'lone parent families', stereotypical images of 'race' and the identification of areas of high delinquency have served to reinforce stereotypes, both in terms of perceptions of offenders and the apparent causes of offending.

Notions of good SIR practice determined that reports should first address the offences and place them in the context of the individual offender, only drawing on those aspects of character and circumstances that may be seen to have direct relevance to the commission of the offence(s). Not only should stereotypes be avoided but also good practice required that any material which might be processed by Magistrates stereotypically should be omitted or presented in a manner that responded to the stereotype. Recommendations should be well argued, programmes for direct work explained in detail and lead logically from the body of the report. If the tariff system was to be allowed to have its fullest potential effect in deterring further offending, recommendations should be based on the least intrusive viable option and lead to the offender having the benefit of all available options including the possibility of moving 'down-tariff'. Where there was a perceived risk of custody the author should address the issue in the SIR, paying particular attention to the criteria which need to be fulfilled and outlining what community alternative programmes may be imposed instead.

In addition to these guidelines for good SIR practice it was acknowledged that there also needed to be a strategic framework for the preparation of reports. In this context, Hazell's (1987) model is representative of models which were identified and adopted at the time of this study. In addition, it was clear that there needed to be effective communication and co-operation between agencies engaged in each local juvenile justice system to promote greater understanding and explore areas of common purpose.

In this chapter I have traced the origins of Social Inquiry Reports showing how they emerged on a 'welfarist' basis in a juvenile justice system that rejected 'welfarism'. I have shown how this led to confusion about the

72

function and purpose of SIRs ans was manifest in widespread inconsistent practice. In the second part of the chapter I reviewed some of the literature relating to SIRs, highlighting the nature of concerns about practice and the resultant prejudicial effect, particularly in relation to Black defendants. Finally, I outlined some principles of good practice which were adopted both in relation to report content and local strategic frameworks.

Clearly, policy and practice has moved on since 1990. Social Inquiry Reports have become Pre-sentence Reports (PSRs) and practice has become the subject of national standards. The purpose of this chapter has been to describe developments up to and including the time of the study. The study itself produced findings which have implications for current practice. These issues will be addressed in the context of the conclusions and recommendations in Part Two.

Having discussed some of the implications of bad SIR practice for Black defendants, I go on in the next chapter to explore the impact of the wider juvenile justice system up to 1990 on Black defendants and demonstrate how prejudice and disadvantage permeates all areas of the system.

5   The juvenile justice
       system and 'race'

In previous chapters I have traced the development of the juvenile justice system, examined court reports, both in terms of their function and variations in practice and highlighted the shifts in emphasis between prevailing ideologies. I have explored notions of racism and anti-racism and considered 'race' in relation to court report practice. In this chapter I shall go on to consider 'race' in the broader context of the juvenile justice system, up to the period of the study; 1990. I shall analyse the seeming over-representation of Black young people at all stages of the juvenile justice system and consider two hypotheses which are currently under discussion as possible explanations for the over-representation of Black people in the system.

Discussions of ethnicity by white society have been viewed with some suspicion by Black people, unsurprisingly, given the way such information has been used against Black people in the past. Given that notions of 'race' are not scientific, the question also arises, whose definitions of ethnicity are to be used? Is a person's ethnicity defined by self-perception, the perception of other people or a curious combination of both? What of dual heritage people?

To group people together as having a common ethnicity can be an unhelpful and unsatisfactory process anyway since it implies a homogeneity which is not only unrealistic but denies individuality and diversity, both in terms of experience and identity. Consequently, there is no universally applied system of ethnic grouping. Instead, a variety of shorthand labels have been adopted with varying degrees of sensitivity - or lack of it - in an attempt to define groups of people.

'Black', as a label, has come to mean different things to different people. In certain settings 'Black' refers to all non-white people. However, this is rejected by some individuals and groups who regard 'Black' as an identification of a more specific grouping of people with shared origins, often in relation to African or Caribbean heritage. This perception has been reinforced by some people whose roots are in the Indian sub-continent who have wished to positively uphold a distinct identity. Other interpretations reject the notion of 'Black' altogether; either the term is regarded as too emotionally charged and threatening, preferring instead to refer to 'coloured' or, alternatively because it is a racist inspired label which serves to compartmentalise the diversity and range of non-white cultures as a homogenous group in convenience to white people who are unprepared to educate themselves and raise their awareness of differing lifestyles and experiences.

The difficulty that exists in defining ethnicity reflects the complexity and artificiality of notions of 'race'. Nonetheless, it is clear that distinctions are drawn between people often on simplistic ideas of skin colour, religion, nationality or cultural origins. It is clear too that these distinctions are utilised as the basis for discrimination. In those circumstances it is important to attempt to reflect those distinctions in order to understand the discriminatory processes which people experience. There is almost an inevitability of insensitivity associated with identifying ethnicity because of the racist use to which it has been put.

The purpose of this study is to gain some understanding of the impact people operating the justice system - largely white people - have on Black people, particularly in relation to sentencing outcomes. It is the perceptions of those who administer the system therefore, which define who is white and who is not. Furthermore, since these are external perceptions they are likely to be less sophisticated, more crudely all-embracing, than the self perception of defendants. For these reasons a relatively simple framework of ethnicity was used, operating at two levels. In the first place, all those defendants who were perceived by SIR authors as non-white are described within the study as 'Black'. To further examine possible distinctions within the 'Black' sample and to avoid compensating errors there was a further sub-division between those who are perceived as having origins in Africa and/or the Caribbean, who are described as 'African-caribbean', and those are were perceived to have origins in the Indian sub-continent who are described as 'Asian'.

In applying these labels to defendants, no assumption is made about the shared experiences of people in any grouping. Rather, these labels are a reflection of actors in the justice system and the compartmentalisation processes they engage in. It is this inclination to group people together, often

75

based on stereotypical assumptions which is problematic to Black defendants and to individualised sentencing since, by definition it denies individuality, instead, categorising people according to a perceived lowest common denominator.

Neutrality of justice?

Within the justice process legal rules are presumed to be neutral. That is to say, they are presumed to 'hold good' at different times, in different regions and across the social divisions of class, gender, 'race', etc. (Worrall, 1990). The judicial oath includes the statement 'do right to all manner of persons, according to the customs and usages of this realm, without fear or favour or ill will'. This ideal is said to be embodied in the Statue of Justice which, in addition to holding the sword of authority and the scales of fairness, is blindfolded to show no fear or favour. However, the principle of equality before the law has been brought into question. The Longford Report (1964) sought to draw attention to the differential treatment people received according to social class. Worrall (1990) identifies the disadvantage experienced by women in the justice system. Similar concerns have been expressed about the inequalities experienced by Black people.

Unnever et al (1980) suggest that 'race' bias may enter the justice process at an early stage and be passed on in many forms including the sentence recommendation in the SIR. Evidence of bias in SIRs has been considered in chapter 4 and receives further attention below as a result of the findings of this study. I wish now to consider what evidence exists in relation to other elements and stages in the juvenile justice system.

Arrests and cautioning

Home Office research conducted in 1975 found that arrests of Black people occurred more frequently than expected in relation to the proportion of Black people in the population as a whole (Stevens and Willis, 1979). Similarly, research in the Metropolitan Police area undertaken by the Policy Studies Institute (1983) showed that a higher proportion of Black young people were likely to be stopped, searched and arrested than were young whites.

Once arrested, the prospect of a young Black person being cautioned are considerably less than their white counterparts (Landau and Nathan, 1983). In 1982, 40% of all juveniles who were classified as white were cautioned by the Metropolitan Police Force in contrast to 26% of those who were classified as Black (GLC, 1984). At face value this appears to indicate disparate practice on the grounds of 'race'. Alternatively, it may be argued that the differential is a reflection of a higher frequency of criminal activity by Black people leading, in turn, to a more rapid progression through the cautioning process.

In Landau and Nathan's (1983) study previous offending was found to be the most predictive variable in the key decision of whether or not to caution. In these circumstances repeated offending by a relatively small number of Black people would lead to a rapid exhaustion of cautioning opportunities and would be reflected by higher prosecution rates. However, since cautions may only be administered in cases where the offence is fully admitted, lower cautioning rates may be indicative of a greater proportion of denials or incomplete admissions in addition to unequal decision making.

Little attention has been given to cautioning rates specifically in relation to Asian young people. However, one study in Leeds (Walker et al, 1989) found that a disproportionately large number of Asian adults who were arrested had no further action taken against them. Clearly there is a need for more research in this area. However, a high incidence of 'no further action' decisions involving adults in one geographic district cannot be presumed to reflect the experiences of Asian people generally and of young Asians in particular.

The contrast between the findings of Walker et al (1989) and those of Nathan and Landau (1983) highlights the dangers inherent in drawing conclusions that the experience of all Black people will be similar. Indeed, whilst over-representation in the justice system seems to apply to Black people generally, over-representation of African-caribbean people is most notable (Mair, 1986). What is clear is that there is growing evidence that Black people are at greater risk of being arrested and are less likely to be cautioned.

Charges and remands

By implication, if there is a greater risk of being arrested and less likelihood of being cautioned, it follows that there must also be a greater overall risk of Black people being processed. However, little research has been conducted to verify this point. Hudson (1989) suggests that in circumstances where more than one charge is applicable to an offence that has been committed, African-caribbean defendants are more likely than whites to face the more serious charge. This may go some way to explain why there is a higher incidence of denials and not guilty pleas entered by African-caribbean people.

Fitzgerald (1991) argues that once charged, Black people are more likely to be remanded in custody before sentencing. A NACRO/ACOP study (1992) noted that whilst remands generally had fallen from 94.19 per month in the first six months of 1989 to 49.8 per month in the first half of 1992, the proportion of Black defendants remanded into custody had not fallen. Indeed, of those remanded to Feltham Young Offenders Institute in the first half of 1992, 74% were recorded as from racial minority groups. In 1981, the Black population in one remand centre amounted to 50% of all inmates; three times the Black population within the catchment area (Home Office, 1981a).

This continuing trend may, in part, reflect Hudson's (1989) observation that Black people are charged with more serious offences than whites but the differential is so marked that this is unlikely to be the only explanation. Home Office statistics (1986) showed that disproportionate numbers of Black people plead not guilty, are then remanded in custody but are subsequently acquitted. This suggests that there is a possibility of an inclination to wrongly arrest or charge Black people. As with arrests and cautions, it appears that Black people are more likely to be charged in circumstances where there is insufficient evidence to convict; that the charges are likely to be more serious than if the defendants were white and, that this is borne out by the level of acquittals.

Sentencing and the penal population

The apparent over-representation and discriminatory treatment of Black people continues to the point of sentence and beyond. A range of studies have consistently detected the over-representation of Black people in custodial institutions. "Ethnic minorities in Borstal" showed a custodial rate for Black people twice as high as for whites (Fludger, 1981). Guest (1984) noted that 25% of young people in the penal population were Black in contrast to a proportion of 10% in the population at large. Between 1988 and 1990 the prison population fell by 4,450 (8.9%) (Home Office, 1990). However, between 1985 and 1989 the percentage of Black prisoners rose from 12.5% to 15% (Home Office, 1989). Thus, whilst there was a reduction in the overall prison population there has been an increase in the proportion of Black prisoners.

There is clear evidence then, that Black people are the subject of discrimination at all stages in the justice process from the point of being stopped and searched through to the imposition of custodial sentences. The effects of this discrimination are manifest in over-representation at several key stages: the point of decision making to charge and to process rather than to caution, in court at the remand stage and in sentencing. Within the Black population it is also apparent that African-caribbean people, most particularly, experience disadvantage. What is not clear is why this over-representation comes about given notions of equality before the law and the neutrality of the rules governing due process.

Theories of over-representation

Two main hypotheses are proposed to explain the over-representation of African-caribbean people Fitzgerald, 1991).

1. African-caribbean people are over-represented in the justice system as a direct consequence of the cumulative effects of discrimination at each of the key stages of the justice system.

2. African-caribbean people are over-represented in the justice system in the same measure that they are over-represented in criminal activity.

Two sub-hypotheses are proposed to explain African-caribbean over-representation in criminal activity.

This level of criminal activity may reflect:-

- the structural position of African-caribbean people in British society, or

- attributes that are unique to African-caribbean people as an 'ethnic' group.

I shall address these hypotheses in reverse order.

Black people and criminal activity

'Attributes', in the context of this hypothesis, has come to mean, a propensity to commit offences and certain types of crime in particular. There exists, a stereotypical view that certain crimes are more likely to be committed by Black people than whites. Most of the 'evidence' to support this view is anecdotal. A large proportion of those who appear in court faced with charges of 'mugging, dipping, carrying a knife and the supply of drugs', it is asserted, are Black people (Crowther, 1991). However, comparative studies of criminal activity between areas with different proportions of Black population would suggest otherwise. Home Office Research (Stevens and Willis, 1979) has suggested that the level of reported crime is unrelated to the proportion of Black people in the local population. Newcastle-upon-Tyne, for example, has a comparatively small Black population but has amongst the highest level of reported crime in the Britain (Stevens and Willis, 1979). It is not possible therefore, to reach firm conclusions about the relative level of criminal activity of Black people, neither is there serious evidence that certain crimes might be regarded as ethnocentric.

This hypothesis is essentially racist in nature since it makes two assumptions. First, it assumes a bio-genetic definition of 'race' such as was prevalent in the nineteenth century but which has since been discredited (see chapter 3). Secondly, it assumes that there is a cultural element that is common to the shared life experience of all African-caribbean people as though they were a homogenous group. This denies the complexity, diversity and multiplicity of moral, religious and life experiences of African-caribbean people.

It has already been noted that it is difficult to define 'Black' because of the diversity of life experience and cultural origins and norms that are apparent and because of the flexibility and movement that exists within and between 'Black' communities. Similarly, African-caribbean people do not represent a single, over-arching set of personal or community characteristics. Consequently it is a sweeping generalisation to suggest that Black people share a common attribute which manifests itself in criminal activity. In the light of this observation this hypothesis can be rejected as being unworthy of serious consideration. Furthermore, it is a dangerous assertion based upon mythology and ignorance which can be used to further undermine the position of Black British people through the perpetuation of stereotypes.

The structural position of Black British people

With regard to the structural position of Black British people in society, Pitts (1988) argues that it should not be surprising that Black people are more criminally active given the level of alienation, marginalisation and deprivation that exists in racist urban communities. Lack of opportunities in education, employment and housing mean that it is difficult for Black people to survive by legitimate reasons. Whilst there might be merit in the argument that Black people are disadvantaged, not only by racist urban communities but by British society as a whole and by the institutions that underpin it, most Black people do not find expression for their struggle through criminal activity. This, then, can only be a partial explanation. A similarly partial explanation may be that Black British people, in consequence of the racism which they experience, find little encouragement to invest in the legitimate activity of society. Thus, as Matza (1964) noted, the absence of positive feelings about societal authority neutralises the moral force of that control.

Instead of asking 'why is Black criminal activity high?', Pitts (1988) expresses surprise that Black criminal activity is not even greater in the light of the impact and effects of racism. Young (1991) links the structural position of Black people and demographic differences in relation to age as key features in explanation of Black criminal activity. It is the combination of deprivation, the urban environment and the relative youthfulness of Black people that leads to higher levels of criminal activity. In both cases the assumption is that Black people are more criminally active. There is little evidence to support this view. Both also ignore the fact that many Black people who enter the justice system have committed no offence.

The many Black people who were unjustly stopped and searched under the 'sus' laws were not dealt with this way because of their increased criminal activity, whether as a result of their environment or youthfulness. Very often they had committed no greater crime than walking in the street. Similarly, those Black people who were arrested and remanded in custody but who were subsequently acquitted, by definition, had committed no crime. The explanations which Young (1991) and Pitts (1988) propose, therefore, are limited. They do nothing to explain the injustices that Black people experience daily because they are presumed to be offenders. What they do is to reinforce the notion that Black people are more criminally active which serves to legitimise the injustice.

Branch (1991) suggests that criminality has less to do with 'race' *per se* but that, coincidentally, Black people display social characteristics in keeping with the overall profile of those who commit offences. That is to say, if a construct was made of the socio-economic and demographic factors common to an offending lifestyle, irrespective of 'race', that construct would bear a marked resemblance to the factors which affect Black people. Put another way, Black people are not inherently more criminal in activity but the social factors which typify the offender include a high proportion of Black people. Most offenders live in working class, inner city areas, are more likely to be unemployed, live in poor quality housing, receive poor education, etc. These mirror the circumstances of many Black people therefore, the argument runs, that they are more likely to figure as offenders. The over-representation of Black people in the justice system therefore, may be a consequence of the disadvantage Black people experience not because they are more criminally active. Alternatively, the over-representation of Black people in the justice system may be a reflection that they 'look' more like offenders - for socio-economic reasons - and consequently are more likely to be regarded as 'appearing' suspicious. In this respect, this latter explanation runs the risk of becoming a self-fulfilling prophecy. Black people share the profile of offenders and are consequently at greater risk of being arrested. Then, because Black people are arrested in greater proportion the profile of offenders becomes increasingly reflective of the structural position of Black people in society, and so come under greater suspicion.

The liberal stance represents agents of justice as acting equally to all people 'without fear or favour' and suggests that if the court have found a defendant guilty, then, on the basis that 'the truth will out', there has been unquestioning confidence in the finding of guilt. Any denial or not guilty plea prior to the finding of guilt was often regarded as a ploy on the part of the defendant to delay the inevitable. However, high profile cases in the late 1980s and 1990s where the Court of Appeal has overturned findings of guilt have brought into question the ability of courts to accurately and impartially determine guilt. In addition, revelations about both the fabrication and withholding of evidence have brought disrepute to the justice system and to those who serve it. Not only have the courts become fallible in the public perception but also miscreant in certain circumstances. Early claims of wrongful arrest, victimisation and miscarriage of justice by Black people have, through loss of public confidence in the justice system, gained credence. Doubt has been cast on the integrity and objectivity of the process and those who administer it. As evidence of injustice has gathered so the plausibility of the hypothesis that Black people engage in greater levels of criminal activity has diminished whilst belief in injustice has increased.

Over-representation as a consequence of discrimination

The hypotheses that suggest that Black people are over-represented in the justice system in the same measure with which they are over-represented in criminal activity locate the problem with Black people. Yet it is apparent that Black people are victims of the system, as demonstrated above. The differential treatment of Black people however, is not a problem of Black people but is a problem of the justice system. I turn, therefore, to consider the hypothesis that over-representation of Black people is a direct consequence of discrimination at each of the key stages of the justice process.

The first stage of the justice process which defendants encounter is at the point of arrest where the agents of the system are the police force. Various writers have commented about the impact of policing policy in relation to Black people and have suggested that that over-representation may be explained by the actions of police officers (See, for example, Benyon, 1986).

Over-representation as a consequence of policing?

The Policy Studies Institute published a series of studies under the heading 'Police and People in London'. In one study in the series Smith and Gray (1983) considered the role of the police in action in which they made observations about the operations and attitudes of police officers. They noted the development of a simplistic and stereotypical equation amongst officers; 'black = criminal = justifiable arrest' (p. 84). It is apparent that if this equation is widespread amongst police officers Black people will be presumed to be engaged in criminal activity because they are Black and will be much more likely to be arrested. Furthermore, if Black people are regarded as inherently criminal it not only justifies the targeting of resources at Black communities, it also impacts upon decision-making following arrest. It follows that if the perception of an arrested Black person is as an offender it makes the decision to charge or to process rather than to caution or take no further action more straightforward.

Pitts (1988) considers accounts of Black people's experiences of individual officers and of the force in general. He argues that because Black people are presumed to be more likely to offend they are placed under great suspicion. He also argues that neighbourhoods predominantly populated by Black people have higher levels of police resources focused upon them. It is the combination of these factors, he says, which leads to larger numbers of Black people being arrested. It is unclear however, whether Pitts is implying that greater police presence leads to the detection of more crimes or if greater police presence brings more Black people under suspicion. The disproportionate levels of not guilty pleas and acquittals of Black defendants suggest the latter.

Fitzgerald (1991) considers the evidence of police stops and arrests of Black people in cases which result in not guilty judgements and speculates that the effect of the arrest itself is criminalising. That is to say that the

83

experience of an unjustifiable arrest may lead to subsequent criminal activity. Such a projection may, at first, appear implausible. However, there are parallels to be found in the school playground where young Black students were unjustifiably accused of disorder. Following repeated accusations some took the view that if they were going to be accused they 'may as well commit the act'. Such unjustifiable arrests, especially if they were to become repeated experiences might easily have a labelling effect insofar as the local community may adopt a 'no smoke without fire' attitude. In this way the individual may be assumed to have acted criminally. Assumptions of this nature are not unique to Black people but, given the propensity to equate Black people with criminal activity, such labels may have a more profound impact when ascribed to Black people. In general terms, people do not react kindly to being arrested. If the arrest is perceived by the defendant to be unjustified feelings of powerlessness and frustration are likely to arise. Those feelings turn to anger, hostility and alienation if unjustified arrests become a repeated experience for the individual. If those individual experiences become shared community experiences the response is likely to be a volatile one, as has been seen in a number of communities.

Recent observations by prominent police officers to the effect that police resources will be targeted at Black communities on the grounds Black people are more likely to commit certain types of offence only serve to fuel the discrimination that already exists. The 'evidence' upon which these assertions are made are consequences of existing disparity in the targeting of resources. If the majority of effort is placed in policing Black communities it is not surprising that an imbalance in arrest statistics will result just as they would if that policing effort was concentrated on wealthy white communities. What follows then is the type of self-fulfilling prophecy which Pearson (1978) describes, where policy results in increased crime statistics which are then used to justify policy. In circumstances where the 'guilt' of Black people is presupposed the decision not to pursue the matter becomes more difficult. Thus, as Hudson (1989) noted, Black people were more likely to be charged with the more serious of two possible offences and similarly, there is less likelihood of Black defendants being cautioned.

It is apparent then, that policing policy may have a direct impact on the over-representation of Black people in the justice system. Beyond the consequences of concious policy is the discrimination that simply arises from institutional racism. The police force is steeped in the dominant culture. Many officers would wish to observe that in carrying out their duties they do so without considerations of 'race' not recognising that this stance in itself is discriminatory. 'A so called "colour-blind" approach may be based on noble sentiments but cannot take account of the complexity of needs and the differences in them' (Aktar, Baldwin and Ghataora, 1995). Without an active consideration of the implications a service may have on Black people that service will inevitably be prejudicial to the interests of Black people. In these circumstances the over-representation of Black people is a problem to the justice system because it is reflective of discrimination from within.

Over-representation of Black people and the courts

Having considered the impact of the police actions in the context of the over-representation of Black people in the justice system I turn now to the role of the courts. The emphasis of previous studies into the operation of courts has largely been on the possibility that sentencing practice influences over-representation of Black people in custodial institutions. Two of the earliest studies concluded that there was no difference in sentencing patterns on the basis of 'race'.

The study conducted by McConville and Baldwin (1982) is widely quoted because it was the first major work to be published. However, both the methodology and the findings have come into question by some authors (for example, Legal Action Group, 1982; Mair, 1986). The study was initiated in 1974 and was primarily concerned with the outcome of cases tried by jury, the role of oral and written statements in Crown Court trials and the determination of guilty pleas. The influence of 'race' and sentencing was addressed through later re-examination of the data. The study was based on four random samples of Crown Court trials comprising:

- contested cases heard in Birmingham in 1975/76:

- guilty plea cases heard in Birmingham in 1975/76:

- contested cases heard in London in 1978/79, and

- guilty plea cases heard in London in 1978/79.

The initial sample of 1476 cases included 239 which involved Black defendants. The research methodology included the process of matching, on a group basis, Black defendants within each sample with white defendants. The criteria for matching included gender, the nature of the offences, age and previous records. The final analysis, therefore, was completed on the basis of 478 sample cases.

The main criticisms associated with this study centred on the fact that it entailed re-processing data collected some years earlier for a different purpose. It was also regarded as unrepresentative of the justice system as a whole because the sample was drawn exclusively from cases heard in Crown Courts. Over 60% of the sample related to hearings in 1975/6 and were thus regarded as dated. Furthermore, since they were drawn from cases in the Crown Courts they related to more serious offences and were not representative of the breadth of criminal cases.

The findings were exposed to further question through close examination of the data. Although the findings asserted that there was no difference in sentencing patterns on the grounds of 'race' it was noted by critics that there was a greater use of custody for Black defendants in three of the four matched groups. In the London 'guilt' plea cases, 53% of Black defendants received custodial sentences compared with 48.5% of whites. In the Birmingham 'guilty' plea cases, the use of custody was marginally greater for whites: 48.2% compared with 46% for Black defendants. In London 'not guilty' plea cases 47.6% of Black defendants were sentenced to custody, marginally more than 45% of whites, whilst in the Birmingham 'not guilty' plea cases 65.6% of Black and 59.2% of white defendants received custodial sentences.

Where there is an over-representation of Black defendants receiving custodial sentences there must be a compensating over-representation of white defendants who had lesser penalties imposed. Interestingly, the study showed the over-representation of whites occurred in relation to probation orders. Three of the four matched groups revealed greater use of probation orders for whites. 8.8% of Black defendants in London 'guilty' plea cases compared with 24.3% of whites; 9% of Black defendants in the Birmingham 'guilty' plea cases compared with 12.3% of whites; 9.5% of Blacks in London 'not guilty' plea cases whilst no white defendants had probation orders imposed and, 3.2% of Black defendants in Birmingham 'not guilty' plea cases where 7.5% of whites received probation orders. Whilst disparity in the use of custodial sentences was relatively small the disparity relating to probation orders was more significant. The interesting observation from this finding is the inference that white defendants were perceived as more deserving of a more 'welfare' orientated disposal than were Black defendants.

It is apparent then, that in their findings, McConville and Baldwin (1982) understate the extent to which Black people are over-represented amongst custodial sentences and under-represented amongst probation orders. Mair (1986) also notes other limitations with this study. First, as noted earlier, it ignores Magistrates' courts where the great majority of criminal cases are heard and which may differ in sentencing outcome from the Crown Court where, he says, 'the professionalism of judges' may be an important factor in treating all offenders equally. Judges, however much expertise they may have in the law, rules of due process and the like, are not immune to subjectivity and prejudice in their rulings. A number of judges have gained fame, if not infamy and notoriety, for the apparent subjectivity and prejudice portrayed by the remarks they have made and the sentences they have imposed. Just as police officers are drawn from a racist society, so too, are judges. The inference, therefore, that Magistrates may be less 'professional' and less 'equal' in their judgements is an unfair one.

Secondly, and more pertinently, Mair (1986) draws attention to the inclusion of all non-white defendants into a single grouping in the study. Any evidence of more severe sentencing towards African-caribbean defendants in the study, for example, may be masked by less severe sentencing of Asian defendants.

Thirdly, attention is drawn to the 'pairing' technique utilised in the study: a device frequently used in social research to reduce the impact of variables within samples. The study was based upon matched groups, that is to say, groups constructed from the overall sample, selected specifically to be similar in nature. Pairing was undertaken on the basis of gender, criminal offence, age and previous record. Mair (1986) suggests that the absence of pairing to take account of employment status represents a shortcoming since courts have shown a greater inclination to incarcerate unemployed defendants. As unemployment is generally higher amongst Black groups sentencing may thus be affected.

There is a broader issue related to 'pairing' which arises. A weakness of 'pairing' as a methodological tool is that it assumes that all variables are known and are amenable to categorisation and denies the possibility of, what might be described as, 'within-category' variables. Mahoney (1991) regards that 'pairing' is an inadequate research technique because, given the samples that are available to researchers, pairs cannot be matched without variables. For example, two defendants charged with theft may be matched for offence seriousness. However, 'within-category' variables such as the value of the property, whether or not it was recovered and the nature and circumstances in which the offence was committed may be lost. This has particular relevance to cases involving Black defendants. In circumstances where the victim is white it is not possible to match the Black defendant in a 'pairing'

87

with a white defendant. There is no equivalent to the impact that an offence committed by a Black person where the victim is white may have on sentencing. Similarly, it is impractical to match certain factors which may have an important bearing on the outcome, such as, for example, the demeanour of the defendant during the court hearing. The range of aggravating and mitigating factors that may apply in criminal cases are imponderable but yet any one of them may feature prominently in determining the outcome. Whilst it was assumed that sentencing was determined by measurable and objective criteria, studies (Parker et al, 1989, Brown, 1990) have shown that many subjective and barely definable factors may have a profound impact on sentencing. Consequently, not only may 'pairing' be inadequate as an eliminator of variables, it may also result in misleading findings.

The second of the early influential studies was that reported by Crow and Cove (1984) involving cases heard in nine courts (four juvenile courts, three Magistrates' courts and two Crown Courts) in London, the Midlands and the north of England between February and June, 1983. In this study 668 cases were surveyed, of which 536 (80.2%) were white; 85 (12.7%) were Black [African-caribbean]; 24 (3.6%) were Asian and 15 (2.2%) were described as 'other'. The ethnicity of eight (1.2%) defendants was unknown. The cases were analysed according to whether the defendant was perceived as white, Black or 'other'.

Comparisons were made between the characteristics of the three groups and differences were noted. The white group had the highest average age and a greater proportion were married. The Black group included the highest level of unemployment and the charges they faced included the fewest robberies and less involving loss but the Black group faced more charges associated with drugs. The 'other' group included the largest proportion of female defendants, the greatest number with no fixed address and had the fewest previous convictions and custodial sentences. However, this group faced charges resulting in the highest amount of loss. Similarity between the groups was noted in relation to type of remand, legal representation, social inquiry reports produced, physical and/or mental illness and mitigating or aggravating factors.

This study found that discharges and community service orders were used more frequently in cases involving Black defendants, whilst probation orders and custodial sentences were more frequently imposed in cases involving whites. Fines were most widely used amongst the 'other' group. From these findings Crow and Cove (1984) concluded that whilst there were variations, they were minor and overall offenders were dealt with similarly.

However, the data suggests that there were important differences in sentencing patterns. White defendants received marginally more custodial sentences than Blacks. Whites were also twice as likely to have a probation order imposed. Black defendants received 30% more community service orders than whites. This also suggests that white defendants were perceived as more amenable to change and more deserving of the 'help' available through probation orders.

Whilst, at first sight, the findings from this study are more encouraging *vis a vis* the over-representation of Black defendants there are some difficulties with the study which diminish its value. First, in 211 cases (nearly one-third of the sample) the eventual sentencing outcome is unknown. More complex cases frequently result in a greater number of adjournments which would take some cases out of the study period. These same complex cases are likely to produce less routine sentencing patterns.

Secondly, the ethnicity of defendants is grouped in such a way that may mask compensatory sentencing patterns. Whilst distinctions are made between white and Black defendants, the 'other' group comprised a combination of people with a variety of ethnic origins as well as those that were unknown. Non-Asian comprised 50% of the 'other' group and those whose origins were not recorded amounted to a further 17%. Information is not given about the ethnicity of the remaining portion of the group and the reader is not informed how dual heritage defendants were defined. This has implications for the findings of the study since the margin of error arising from the inappropriate grouping of defendants' ethnicity may significantly affect the data.

Thirdly, data for this study was collated from different courts with different sentencing powers but were analysed as a single group. The absence of custodial sentencing powers for under 14s in the juvenile court may influence the findings. Any over-representation of Black and 'other' defendants under 14 years of age would have the effect of reducing the custody rate for non-whites. The demographic trend at the time of the study is very likely to have produced precisely this feature of over-representation of under 14 year old Black defendants appearing in court.

These two studies pioneered the research of 'race' and sentencing at a point in time when there was official reluctance to acknowledge the possibility of racism influencing outcomes. Their importance therefore, is in having paved the way for other, subsequent, studies specifically designed to examine the matter utilising refinements of the methodology and techniques of the early studies. Consequently, there are interesting contrasts in findings and methods between earlier and later studies. I shall look in detail at three of the later studies and consider in brief three others.

Mair's (1986) pilot study was focused on magistrates' courts in Leeds and Bradford and surveyed 1173 cases between September and November 1983. 81% of the sample cases involved male defendants who were sentenced before February 1984. The aim of the pilot was to examine the service Black defendants from probation officers in relation to whites thus the survey included a range of measures including sentencing outcomes. 88.7% of the sample was white whilst 5.5% and 5.2% were Black and Asian respectively. Fifty cases involving Black defendants and 50 involving Asians were matched with white defendants by age, gender, offence type, the number of previous convictions and the most serious previous disposal.

Similarities were noted in SIR recommendations but there was a significant difference found in referrals by the courts for SIRs. Reports were requested differently for whites in each of the matched groups: 30% of cases involving whites and 47% of Blacks were adjourned for reports in one matched group, whilst 40% of whites and 31% of Asians had adjournments for reports in the other. Mair (1986) could offer no explanation for this variance and it is an area worthy of further investigation in relation to current PSR practice.

With regard to sentencing, minority ethnic groups were again found to be less likely to receive probation orders than whites: 6.3% of Blacks and 3.2% of Asians compared with 11.6% of whites. However, Asian defendants were more likely to receive community service orders: 12.9% compared with 6.7% (whites) and 7.8% (Blacks). Just 0.3% separated all three ethnic groups in relation to the imposition of custodial sentences. These differences do not disappear through the matching process which, together with the observation that recommendations were similar between groups Mair (1986) suggests that disparity is a product of the court and not of probation officers.

Although the minority study surveyed 1173 cases, the small proportion involving African-caribbean and Asian defendants (10.7%) produces some difficulties which the author acknowledges. The study does distinguish between African-caribbean and Asian defendants but no explanation is given of how dual heritage defendants were grouped.

Pimm and Lines (1987) study of 225 cases heard in all courts in Birmingham between 10 and 21 March 1986 also found differences in sentencing across 'race' boundaries. Of the sample, 75.7% were white and 24.3% were described as Black. In this case the 'Black' group included all non-white defendants. The cases were not matched but the fact that this study also considers cases involved in courts with different sentencing powers for different age groups may have some impact on the findings.

It was found that whites were more likely to receive probation/supervision orders (25.6% compared with 20.4%) and were more than twice as likely to be fined (12.5% compared with 5.6%). Black defendants received fewer community service orders (9.3% compared with 16.1%) but were much more likely to receive a custodial sentence (48.2% compared with 30.3%).

In view of these findings, the authors tested for differences in the commission of serious offences (sexual offences, robbery, murder, assault or wounding). They found that serious offences were twice as common amongst white than Black defendants: 8% of whites were charged with serious offences compared with 4% of Blacks. They also noted that Black defendants sentenced to custody were significantly less likely to have served previous custodial sentences: 36.8% of Black defendants had previous custodial sentences compared with 58.3% of whites.

In relation to SIR recommendations, it was found that a similar proportion of Black and white defendants had community alternative recommendations made but, overall, fewer were adopted in cases involving Black defendants (42.9%) than whites (58.3%). In those cases where the recommendations were not adopted, 50% of Black defendants received custodial sentences compared with 35.5% of whites. These findings may reflect the scenario highlighted earlier whereby report authors, in their sensitivity to the increased possibility of a custodial sentence in cases involving Black defendants may have been inclined to recommend community alternative programmes in circumstances which, were the defendant white, would not have been warranted.

There was a higher rate of recommendation of probation/supervision orders made in respect of white defendants (38.9% compared with 33.3%) and significantly more recommendations were adopted for white (60.7%) than Black defendants (42.9%). When recommendations for probation/supervision orders were not adopted, 81.8% of Black defendants received custodial sentences compared to 50% of whites.

Similar findings were noted in relation to recommendations for community service orders. Only 25% were adopted where defendants were Black compared with 53.7% of whites. Where recommendations were not adopted the imposition of custodial sentences was similar for both groups. In those cases where no recommendation was made, all Black defendants received custodial sentences compared to 57.1% of white defendants.

These findings suggest disparity of sentencing on the grounds of 'race'. The inclusion of all minority ethnic defendants in one group may have led to an over-representation of one sub-group and a compensating under-representation of another. However, there is significant evidence here of disparity of sentencing across all minority ethnic groups.

Voakes and Fowler (1989) studied 633 cases in Magistrates' and Crown Court in Bradford between April and June 1987. 526 (79.3%) involved white defendants, 69 (10.4%) were Asian, 30 (4.5%) were African-caribbean, 23 (3.5%) were described as 'mixed race' and 15 (2.3%) were of unknown origin. When consideration was given to the nature of the offences, previous convictions, remand type, employment and the age and gender of the defendants it was calculated that white defendants were at the greatest risk of custody. However, the findings showed that Asian and African-caribbean offenders were more likely to be fined or have custodial sentences imposed and were less likely to be placed on probation or community service orders.

In particular, it was found that custodial sentences were more frequently imposed on African-caribbeans in Magistrates' courts. 30% of African-caribbean defendants received sentences of imprisonment compared with 27.5% of Asians and 21.5% of whites. Whilst in the context of community alternative sentences 4.5% of Asians received community service orders, 13.5% of African-caribbean defendants were so sentenced.

Voakes and Fowler (1989) also analysed a sample of 489 SIRs, of which 404 (82.6%) related to whites, 42 (8.6%) to Asians, 24 (4.9%) related to African-caribbean defendants and 19 (3.9%) were related to defendants described as 'mixed race'. From this sample it was established that probation officers were more likely to make no recommendation in cases involving African-caribbean defendants. However, this was partly explained by a greater proportion of not guilty pleas entered by African-caribbean people and cases where appointments were not kept.

There was a similar level of recommendation of community service orders for Asian (36%) and white (35%) defendants but less for African-caribbeans (25%). As already noted, the lower incidence of community service order recommendations is reflected in sentencing levels.

Inferences of disparity of sentencing on the grounds of 'race' arising from these studies may only be made tentatively, not least in those studies which become confused by drawing on cases heard in courts with different sentencing powers or where age restricts sentencing options. Nevertheless, they add collective weight to the hypothesis that African-caribbeans are over-represented in the justice system as a direct consequence of the cumulative effects of discrimination at each of the key stages of the justice system. Most of the studies have been centred on adult courts; some combined adult and juvenile courts. Few studies have focused on juvenile courts alone. Since age is a factor in sentencing (Mair, 1986) even the tentative suggestion of disparity made through the findings of these studies cannot be assumed to be transferable to children and young people. Three studies which were conducted specifically in juvenile courts however, would seem to suggest that disparity does exist to a similar degree in cases involving young people.

Tipler's studies (1985, 1986) would suggest that there is disparity of sentencing on the grounds of 'race' in relation to young offenders. His first study, conducted in Hackney between October 1984 and March 1985 surveyed 343 cases heard in the juvenile court involving 269 defendants, 89.2% of whom were male. Tipler (1985) found that white defendants were more likely to receive conditional discharges (33% compared with 26%) and fines (32% compared with 29%) than Black defendants. In the context of this study all non-white defendants were grouped together with those whose ethnicity was unknown. With regard to every other disposal except s.7(7) care orders, Black defendants were over-represented. However, it should be noted that the numbers involved in this study are small and are open to inaccuracy because of the inclusion of those whose ethnicity was unknown.

Tipler's second study - building on the first - included cases heard between October 1984 and March 1986. This study considered issues relating to cautioning, pleas and findings of guilt as well as sentencing outcomes. In this study, as with the first, the sample was divided into two groups, white and Black; the latter including all non-white defendants and those whose ethnicity was unknown.

With regard to comparisons of offences, motor vehicle offences featured more prominently amongst the white group (33% compared with 13%), whilst burglary, robbery and offences relating to drugs and weapons featured more highly amongst the Black group. All other offences were broadly similar for both groups.

There was also similarity in relation to most sentencing options. However, more whites were fined (36% compared with 31%) and significantly more Black defendants received custodial sentences (12% compared with 7%). Again, however, the sample size is small and the author concedes that the findings had no statistical significance.

Berry (1984) surveyed 1217 cases appearing before Nottingham juvenile court during a 15 month period. The findings report that Black defendants were twice as likely to receive custodial sentences than white defendants and that neither the nature of the charges nor the previous criminal records accounted for the difference (NACRO, 1987, p. 2).

The most comprehensive study to examine whether 'race' is a factor influencing the sentences imposed in the Crown Courts is that conducted by Hood (1992). Based on a large sample of cases it revealed a 'complex and disturbing pattern of racial differences in the resort to custody, the length of sentences and the choice of alternative punishments' (Hood, 1992).

The study was carried out in six Crown Courts served by West Midlands Police. It was based on an analysis of all information available in relation to all minority ethnic males convicted and sentenced at these courts in 1989 and an equivalent number of white males. In addition cases involving all women sentenced in these courts during the period were analysed separately and the outcomes compared. In total 3327 cases were analysed.

Minority ethnic defendants constituted 28% of the males sentenced; two and a half times greater than their proportion in the population at large. African-caribbeans were generally over-represented in the courts. Of the sample, the proportion of African-caribbean defendants sentenced to custody was 56.6%, eight percentage points higher than whites (48.4%). Asians were sentenced to custody less often (39.6%). Hood (1992) noted that there were significant differences in the sentencing patterns displayed by judges; three sentences fewer Blacks to custody than whites, eight were described as 'relatively even-handed' (p. 195) and five sentenced a much higher proportion of African-caribbeans than whites to custody. Assistant Recorders were found to be relatively lenient compared with more senior and experienced Circuit Judges and Recorders. Optimistically, this may reveal that racism is diminishing with each generation of sentencers. The alternative observation may be that Assistant Recorders had not acquired the practices of their seniors at this time.

A comparison of the circumstances of each case showed that disparity of sentencing could not be explained by the characteristics of the cases. There were differences in the type but not the seriousness of offending. However, although fewer African-caribbean defendants had no previous convictions a higher proportion of whites had eight or more. Also more African-caribbean defendants pleaded not guilty and opted for trial by jury, a consequence of which was that there were fewer SIRs produced for African-caribbean defendants. The smaller proportion of Asian defendants sentenced to custody was perceived to be reflective of lesser involvement in criminal acts.

After consideration had been given to the material circumstances of the cases it was calculated that male African-caribbean defendants were 5% more like to be sentenced to custody than whites. This represented 24

94

African-caribbean males being sentenced to custody in 1989 who would not have been if issues of 'race' had no effect on sentencing.

Of great significance was the finding that the greatest difference in the proportion of African-caribbean and white males sentenced to custody was in the medium seriousness band. In other words, an African-caribbean male was much more likely to be sentenced to custody having committed an offence of medium seriousness than was a white male. In these courts and at this time, therefore, it is apparent that the threshold for custodial sentences was lower for African-caribbeans than for whites.

Differences were noted in the practices of each of the courts with greater disparity of sentencing occurring in some courts than others. Differences were also noted in the length of custodial sentences imposed. A significantly higher proportion of African-caribbean and Asian defendants received sentences of over three years and the average length of sentences was also longer. Some of this difference might be explained by the higher proportion of not guilty pleas entered by African-caribbean defendants.

Across the range of tariff sentences African-caribbeans were placed higher up the scale than whites. They were more likely to be given a fully suspended prison sentence than whites and less likely to be given probation or community service orders. Asian defendants, on the other hand, were generally given less intrusive sentences. They were also less likely to be placed on probation than whites but they were more likely to be fined or conditionally discharged.

Sentencing differences were less apparent in cases involving women or males under 21 years. Differences were noted in Police actions which, it was suggested, may play a greater role in the prosecutions brought against African-caribbeans at the Crown Court than it does for white and Asian defendants. The manner in which defendants came to notice formed a significant difference and reflected the targeting of police resources on Black people and communities. African-caribbean defendants were much more likely to be known to the police and the court appearance much more likely to arise from stop and search, 'discovery' or some other police initiated action.

The cumulative effect of research findings is to suggest that African-caribbeans are over-represented in the justice system as a result of discrimination at each stage of the justice process. Some research has been less than conclusive for reasons already identified: the possibility of compensating errors where ethnicity has been insufficiently defined; findings masked by inclusion of data from courts/age groups where different sentencing powers are in operation, etc. Questions arise about the possibility of in-built 'race' bias in methodology too. The extent to which matched pairs carries implicit imbalance because of the effect of crimes committed by Black defendants against white victims is an issue. So too, is the impact of pairing on the basis of previous sentencing in the light of increasing evidence of disparity of sentencing between people of different ethnicity. All these factors raise scope for doubt. Nevertheless, with each new study comes increasing evidence and the impact of the Hood report (1992) has been significant. Even so, unequal treatment which is apparent in one age group does not confirm unequal treatment in another.

The emphasis of this study is upon juveniles. Very little research has been conducted exclusively with this age group and consequently, although the indications point in support of the hypothesis, the level of certainty that exists is even lower. There is urgent need for further research in this area, particularly taking into account the changes that have occurred in the first half of the 1990s. There is a danger of issues of 'race' becoming less prominent as a research issue because of the apparent attention that has been given over the last ten years and the many other issues that have arisen more recently. There is a sense in which much has been said about 'race' in the justice system when little has been done. This leads to the possibility of fatigue around the issue and resultant diminution of support for further research just when successful conclusions could be built on the foundations that have been laid. Post-modernism and the 'been there, seen it, got the T-shirt' philosophy should not detract from the on-going issues, at the centre of which is 'race' and the youth justice system.

Over-representation as a consequence of the juvenile justice process

In this chapter I have given consideration to 'race' in the justice system. I have explored the seeming over-representation of Black people and tested out evidence in support of two hypotheses. I have argued that although the justice system is deemed to be neutral, discriminatory practice occurs in each stage in the process which leads to the over-representation, most particularly, of African-caribbean people. The evidence, without being conclusive, is nonetheless compelling. Similarly, I have argued that to assert that Black criminal activity is greater and leads to over-representation is to deny the evidence that discrimination exists and risk its perpetuation. If, however, discrimination exists it is important to determine the source of such practices as a prelude to engage in its elimination.

Bean (1971) has noted that responsibility for the over-representation of African-caribbeans in the justice system has traditionally been placed with

Magistrates. However, there is no evidence to suggest that other players in the system are any less responsible. Sentencers represent just one group who operate within the system and scrutiny of all roles is required if discrimination is to be eliminated.

Sentencing of an offender comes about as the culmination of a sometimes lengthy and complex process which begins with an allegation that an offence has been committed. That process involves a number of agencies and individuals, each of whom impacts upon the final outcome. In the first place a decision has to be made whether or not to arrest. Further decisions will be made which will determine how far the case will progress through the system. During the course of this progress documentation will be collated detailing the circumstances of the offence. The 'facts of the matter' will be the subject of deliberation by a variety of groups including police officers, social workers, probation officers, education department officials, defence solicitors, Crown Prosecution solicitors, etc. Each will be informed by their own value base and, with a mixture of conscious and subconscious consideration, will make judgements about the case and the defendant. The judgements formed by any or all of these individuals and groups may then influence the final outcome. Consequently, responsibility for disparity of sentencing and the unequal treatment of Black people may be placed on any or all of the persons involved.

It is not possible to consider all stages or individual roles that operate within the system in this study. The purpose of this study is to consider specifically, the role of social workers, particularly insofar as that role is manifest in SIR production.

In Part One of this book - 'The Backdrop' - I have examined the nature and origins of racism in contemporary Britain and have noted that attempts at anti-racism have been patchy both in application and success. I have traced changing ideologies through the development of the juvenile justice system in England and Wales and have noted that considerations of 'race' are absent. I have examined the literature relating to SIR practice and have shown how Black defendants can be disadvantaged by the content of court reports just as they would appear to be disadvantaged by the justice system as a whole. The effect of this disadvantage has been to leave Black people differentially placed in relation to whites in the justice system. I have considered the various hypotheses and have found that whilst evidence in support of the notion that the over-representation of African-caribbean people is a consequence of the cumulative effects of discrimination at all key stages of the justice system is not conclusive, it is no less compelling.

In Part Two - 'Negative Images' - I shall focus first on the operation of the juvenile justice system as it was in 1990. I shall build a profile of the cases heard in Wolverhampton, analyse sentencing outcomes and explore court report practice. Finally, I shall make recommendations for future practice bearing in mind the legislative changes that have occurred.

Part Two
Negative Images

6 Wolverhampton, social services and the local juvenile justice system

In Part One, I began by exploring the emergence of racism in contemporary Britain and tracing the development of the juvenile justice system in England and Wales followed by an examination of the changing ideologies and consideration of a sentencing tariff. I then reviewed studies that have been undertaken in relation to three characteristics of the justice system under the heading of the treatment of Black people: SIRs, the over-representation of African-caribbean people in the justice system and disparity in sentencing.

In Part Two, attention is focused upon the detail of the study conducted in Wolverhampton. Chapter 6 describes the Borough of Wolverhampton, the prevailing structure of the social services department at the time of the study and the operation of the local juvenile justice system. In chapter 7 I shall outline the research methodology employed in the quantitative and qualitative components of the study before presenting the findings in chapters 8 and 9 respectively. Finally, I shall draw conclusions and make recommendations in the context of changing policy and practice.

Wolverhampton

The Metropolitan Borough of Wolverhampton comprises three towns - Wolverhampton, Bilston and Wednesfield - with a population of 242,190 (Census, 1991). It is one of seven Metropolitan Boroughs which together comprised the former county of West Midlands. Wolverhampton is situated at the north-west edge of a conurbation which extends virtually unbroken in a south-easterly direction as far as Coventry, 36 miles away.

Being on the fringes of the 'Black Country', Wolverhampton has a historical association with heavy industry; in particular, the steel and coal industries. However, since the late 1970s these industries have been in decline, producing high levels of unemployment. In line with that decline, the area experienced a downturn in economic activity and wealth which, in the mid 1990s, is only now beginning to be reversed.

It is because of Wolverhampton's industrial base that the town has a two hundred year tradition of attracting migrant workers; first from other parts of the British Isles and, more recently, from Europe and the Commonwealth. By 1981, the Black people accounted for 15.5% of the town's population. Strong traditions of white, working class culture representative of England, Ireland, Scotland and Wales were fused over years into fiercely territorial community lifestyles. A complex diversity of Black traditions, experiences, lifestyle and cultural expression drawn from four continents have been superimposed on that hybrid of white tradition. In consequence, contemporary Wolverhampton is genuinely a multi-cultural and multi-faith community. It is not, however, without its tensions. The shared experience of relative poverty has not served to unite communities but has served to divide them; sometimes fired by the racism inherent in local political representation over the last three decades.

Wolverhampton Social Services Department

Social services departments were established in 1971 (Local Authorities Act, 1970) with a requirement to produce a ten year plan for development. In Wolverhampton, the plan was produced in 1972 and was the basis for the development of service delivery in the borough. In the mid-1980s the Social Services Committee developed a further Five Year Plan to take account of service delivery in the light of changing demographic changes. Simultaneously, the department was restructured on a design intended to provide generic social work services in geographically based teams. These teams would comprise all fieldwork, residential and day care resources for the locality, supported by divisional and departmental management teams.

The new structure brought about the creation of four geographic divisions, each comprising three community teams responsible to a Community Team Manager. Each division was headed by a Divisional Director who, in turn, was responsible to the Director of Social Services. The divisions had three functions,

a) direct management of services,

b) intra- and inter-divisional co-ordination and,

c) service development.

Departmental management, headed by the Director of Social Services, comprised two assistant directors; one with responsibility for resource and information management and the other for research, planning and staff development. The functions of the departmental management group were fourfold: forward planning, staff development, monitoring of services and finance and administration.

Certain of the department's resources had borough-wide, rather than divisionally based operations. To accommodate these resources a matrix structure was established in which each divisional director had borough-wide responsibility for each of four client groups: children and families, disability and mental illness, older people and learning disabilities.

The Adolescent Services Team, comprising the Juvenile Court Liaison Section, the Juvenile Justice Team and Girls' and Young Women's Worker, had responsibility for servicing the juvenile justice system in Wolverhampton. The Juvenile Court Liaison Team represented the department ,in the juvenile court and the Juvenile Liaison Panel. The Juvenile Justice Team provided a consultancy service for community team social workers, serviced the FSP and CAP meetings, undertook assessments and prepared reports in support of alternative to custody recommendations and engaged in direct work with offenders. Girls' and young women's work ran parallel to the Juvenile Justice Team functions in acknowledgement of the fact that there was a greater risk of deviant behaviour resulting in recourse to the care system. Duties relating to the care and supervision of children and young people and SIR preparation was undertaken within community teams.

The local juvenile justice system

The Borough of Wolverhampton is served by one juvenile court, one police division, one probation service office and borough council departments largely sharing common geographic boundaries. Following the arrest of a young person it was the practice in 1990 - at the time of the study - for the police to refer the person to the Juvenile Liaison Panel unless a decision had been made to:

a) administer an informal warning or caution,

b) charge and bail the juvenile to appear in court, or,

c) keep the juvenile in custody for production at the next court session.

The Juvenile Liaison Panel comprised representatives of 'G' Division - West Midlands Police, Social Services Department (2), Education Department and the Probation Service. Discussion of individual cases took place at weekly meetings, following which recommendations were made to caution the juvenile, administer an informal warning, take no further action or process the case. In circumstances where the police were unable to accept the recommendation, a review process was in place to reconsider the facts of the matter and, if possible, to resolve differences of opinion about the most desirable action. In the final outcome, ultimate authority for decision-making rested with the police.

In cases resulting in a court appearance, should the Magistrates request a Social Inquiry Report, the report would be prepared by the probation service or the social services department. The probation service would produce the report were the juvenile aged fourteen or over and was not already known to social workers. In other cases involving juveniles aged under 14 the request would go to the community team responsible for the area in which the young person lived.

In those cases where the SIR author believed the juvenile to be at risk of 'care or custody', it was departmental policy for a Family Support Panel (FSP) to be convened to discuss the case. The FSP was generally chaired by the divisional director and comprised a core group of social workers drawn from the division, community team and the Juvenile Justice Section. In addition, representatives from within the department or from other agencies who had a knowledge of the juvenile may be invited to attend. The purpose of the FSP was to assess the individual needs of the juvenile, identify any service input that may be required, formulate a framework and recommendation for the SIR consistent with the needs service input that were identified.

FSPs, however, were only appropriate where there was a perceived risk of 'care or custody'. As a result, two divisions in the department established Community Alternative Panels (CAPs) as informal gate-keeping mechanisms operating irrespective of the perceived level of risk of 'care or custody'. These CAPs were designed to act as support networks for SIR authors and to give consideration to individual cases in an attempt to implement consistent report writing standards and recommendations throughout each division. Similar gate-keeping mechanisms operated in the probation service and were eventually to become an integrated system.

Juvenile justice and departmental policy

Discussion about differing ideologies in juvenile justice has been discussed in chapter 3. The purpose here is to outline the policy of the department as specified in the 'Manual of Policy and Procedures' (WMBC, 1987). The policy of the department was (and remains) essentially a diversionary policy. That is to say, the department endeavours to divert children and young people from court, 'care or custody' and, ultimately, from offending. It seeks to do this by adopting a practice based upon a systems management approach with minimal intervention directly with offenders.

System management is a process whereby the department intervenes with the decision making processes of the justice system. Locally, this entails the involvement in discussions in the Juvenile Liaison Panel and the juvenile court, with a view to bringing influence to bear in order to divert juveniles from the stigmatising and labelling effects of each successive stage of the justice system. In each case, the departmental representative is expected to advocate the least intrusive course of action appropriate to the circumstances of the case. For example, in the case of a first time offender whose case had been referred to the Juvenile Liaison Panel, the department's representatives would be urging that some other action was taken which would avoid a court appearance, thus allowing the impact of detention and arrest to have a deterrent effect upon the young person and bring about modification in her/his behaviour.

In addition to performing a system management role the Juvenile Justice Team also undertook intervention in those circumstances where it was required, usually as an alternative to a custodial sentence. In circumstances where a defendant was perceived to be at risk of 'care or custody' the FSP or CAP may initiate the an assessment with a view to supporting the recommendation of a specified activity order in the SIR. This would culminate in the preparation of a separate but complementary court report prepared by a member of the Juvenile Justice Team detailing the assessment and outlining a tailor-made programme of intervention appropriate to the needs and circumstances of the individual. Direct work with offenders was undertaken by the Juvenile Justice Team on the basis of a minimum intervention policy in cases where recommendations for intermediate treatment requirements or, more usually, specified activity orders were adopted by the court.

Discussion in chapter 3 included consideration of a sentencing tariff based upon a graduated system of sentencing options. As the defendant progressed through the tariff with each successive court appearance so the intrusiveness of the sentence imposed increases resulting, ultimately, in a loss of liberty. A philosophy of diversion is based on the twin principles of :

- most young people grow out of crime and,

- that maturation process should not be adversely affected by the over zealous imposition of sanctions.

It is nonetheless important to respond to offending behaviour with a clear statement about its unacceptability. However, such rapid progression through the tariff that does not allow each level of sanctions to have an impact may be counter-productive to the long term aim of diversion from offending. On the contrary, it may serve to reinforce the young persons negative self-perceptions through the labelling process. In this respect, pre-court diversion acts as an important preliminary tariff in discouraging offending behaviour without recourse to a court appearance, with all the stigmatisation that that entails.

The notion of self-image is important here especially in relation to 'race' since if accelerated progression through the tariff occurs most often with Black defendants, it is likely that Black children and young people will perceive themselves as inherently deviant. It is for this reason that it is important to ascertain whether there is disparity of sentencing on the grounds of 'race' in order that the issue is addressed and efforts made to avoid such labelling processes.

Accordingly, the Adolescent Services Team has been engaged in recording and analysing outcomes in the juvenile court since 1987. This process was initially undertaken manually. As a result it was limited in scope. Although it shed some light on sentencing patterns it was only possible to speculate tentatively about the causes of the trends that were noted.

In particular, questions arose about the sentencing of African-caribbean defendants who, in 1987, comprised 33% of all those given custodial sentences (WMBC, 1988). This was in stark contrast to the composition of the population of 16 year olds in Wolverhampton, of which just 10% were African-caribbean (Wolverhampton Careers Service, 1988). Even when considered in relation to the ethnicity of those appearing in court - which included disproportionate numbers of African-caribbeans - a custody rate of one-third seemed excessive. Whilst 1 in 8 white defendants were given a custodial sentence, the proportion was 1 in 7 for Asian defendants and 1 in 3 for African-caribbeans (WMBC, 1988). Whilst this preliminary analysis indicated disparity it gave no explanation of the causes.

Although it was possible to make some adjustments in the way information was recorded and the range of data gathered it was still not possible to undertake sufficiently comprehensive research to bring about an understanding of the causes for the trends that were being observed. It was recognised that that it was necessary to broaden the terms of the research to test hypotheses relating to the reasons for the disparity. This would include consideration of the contribution that SIR authors might make through their discriminatory practice. Without taking on board that extra dimension within the study there would be no evaluation of social work practice and no basis from which to make recommendations for change. In short, it would have been an opportunity lost.

As a result of these considerations this research study has been designed to analyse sentencing outcomes through a quantitative analysis and, simultaneously, a qualitative analysis of SIRs. In the course of the next chapter I shall out line the parameters of the study and described the research methodology employed in relation to each of the analyses. I shall then present the findings of the studies in the following two chapters.

7   Research methodology

During the course of this chapter I shall re-state the object of the study and identify the main hypotheses. Following discussion of about the choice of a case study approach and the validity of case studies as a method of social research *per se*, I shall outline the methodology employed in each of the quantitative and qualitative analyses.

The object of the study

Mention has been made earlier of previous research undertaken by the Adolescent Services Team in relation to sentencing in the local juvenile court. One of the consequences of research programmes, it seems, is that they often pose more questions than they answer. Such was the experience of the Adolescent Services Team following the initial monitoring exercises. Whilst the results of those studies were valuable in creating a profile of sentencing patterns which seemed to suggest that African-caribbean defendants were over-represented in high-tariff sentences, such suggestions were only tentative and offered no explanation of causation. A study in greater depth was required if a deeper understanding of sentencing patterns and the effects of racism in operation was to be gained.

This study then, was undertaken in order to test out hypotheses which had arisen from previous monitoring exercises, namely:

1. There is disparity in sentencing according to ethnicity.

2. This disparity is manifest in higher tariff sentencing of Black defendants

3. The reasons for this disparity, in part, reflects discriminatory social work practice as revealed in social inquiry reports.

The case study as a research method

In employing a case study technique it was recognised that the published findings would have two audiences; a local audience, which might have a particular interest in the operation of the justice process in Wolverhampton specifically and, a wider audience, which might have an interest in the justice system more broadly. Whilst it is apparent that a case study may serve the purpose of the local audience it may not be appropriate for the wider audience in portraying national trends. This study claims only to give some insight into the way a particular local justice system was working at one moment in time.

There are two main criticisms of the case study approach (Hall et al, 1978, p. 13). First, that it is not employed in a sufficiently rigorous way to advance theory. Secondly, it does not lend itself to generalisation, however carefully undertaken. Hence, it can never form the basis of a theory.

There has, however, been a tradition built up over the years of the utilisation of case studies as a means of developing understanding of the justice process (see, for example, Baldwin and McConville, 1982; Crow and Cove, 1984; Mair, 1986; Hood, 1992, etc.). Located within this tradition, the aim of this study is to increase understanding of the operation of the local justice system in Wolverhampton at a particular point in time. Such understanding cannot be assumed to reflect the operation of the justice system nationally or at any other moment in history. However, it is hoped that other studies will be conducted in other areas and, by building upon the existing tradition, they may have a cumulative effect in developing greater understanding of the processes at work in the justice system as a whole.

Despite the criticisms they identify, Hall et al (1978) state that if there is a reasonably similar set of cases to provide the opportunity for some cautious comparison, the case study approach is justifiable. The advantage of the case study is that it allows for detailed examination of a particular process as a means of developing understanding of one case in isolation from others. In this setting the case study allows for examination of the justice as it impacted on the lives of children and young people in Wolverhampton in 1990.

Methodology

In order to test out these hypotheses a study was designed in two parts. First, a quantitative study was undertaken of all cases heard in Wolverhampton Juvenile Court in 1990. Details relating to each case were collected by Social Services Department Court Officers and collated on case information record sheets for entry on the database for analysis. These data included details of current proceedings, antecedents and sentencing outcomes in addition to the age, 'race' and gender of the offender.

Matched groups were not used in this study, in part because of the small sample involved but also because of the limitations apparent in the pairing process. As noted earlier, the effectiveness of 'pairing' as a technique for eliminating variables has been brought into question (Mahoney, 1991) particularly since studies conducted by Parker et al (1989) and Brown (1990) have shown how the decision making process of the court ids often dependant upon social 'constructs' of individual defendants' attitudes and circumstances as much as the 'facts' of the matter. Clearly, each case presents its own unique characteristics which are limitless and, because of the apparent subjectivity of the sentencing process, they may be unknown to the researcher. Furthermore, I have argued that cases involving Black defendants carry features which are likely to be impossible to 'match', especially in those circumstances where the victim of the offence was white. Offences committed by white defendants are unlikely to evoke the same response from a largely white Magistracy as those committed by Black defendants involving white victims. In making this case I would argue that comparative case studies are inevitably flawed in a way that is not resolved through 'pairing' and that any findings may only be presented speculatively.

Using the data collected a profile of sentencing patterns was established which formed the basis of comparison according to offence type, remand status, the number of previous offences and court appearances, etc. Thus consideration was given to the material factors which might lead to differential sentencing.

For the purpose of this study defendants were placed into one of three groups: white, African-caribbean and Asian. Dual heritage defendants were included in the African-caribbean or Asian group as appropriate dependant upon the racial origin of their Black parent. Although the resulting Asian group was relatively small in number it was deemed preferable to retain three groups for analysis in order to avoid the possibility of masked results.

Social inquiry report analysis

In order to test the third hypothesis a qualitative analysis of a sample of 123 court reports was undertaken relating to cases heard in the same court during the same period. The challenge related to this component of the study was in devising a form of analysis which was not impressionistic and which accommodated the perspectives of Magistrates as receivers and processors of the material contents.

In considering the nature of the analysis attention was paid to the means by which court reports communicate information to sentencers. Silverman (1985) argues that words are not a preliminary to an investigation of reality but are a reality in their own right. Similarly, Cicourel (1964) and Blumer (1956) outlined the importance of words - adjectives in particular - in conveying positive or negative images. Words then, are not value-free but value-laden. The words which court report authors use to portray defendants are important because they transmit value judgements as part of the process of being descriptive.

A system was devised which combined analysis of the use of language and the way that language is perceived by sentencers. All of the terms used in the report sample to describe defendants were extracted and collated in documentary form. The lists of descriptive terms were sent to 145 participating Magistrates representing three Juvenile Benches. Each Magistrate was asked to give a score on a five point grid reflecting whether the description conveyed a positive or negative image of the defendant. By aggregating the scores from the returned lists it was possible to determine the overall positivity or negativity of the defendant as conveyed by each term. At this point scores were allotted to court reports according to the descriptive terms used. A comparison of report scores was then undertaken to assess whether there were any differences between the images conveyed of defendants according to racial origin. (A comprehensive description of this process follows.)

Analysis of causative factors

Harris and Webb (1987) were less concerned with the values transmitted by language than the power imbalance between report authors and defendants as it was reflected in the causative factors for offending identified by authors and outlined in reports. One of the functions of the court report is to identify a range of issues present in a particular case and develop strategies intended to address those issues. Harris and Webb (1987) identified nine key issues which they found report authors used as 'coathooks' to explain offending behaviour. These issues included perceptions of:

- deviant family norms
- problematic parental disciplining
- disruption caused by separation
- absence from school
- parental criminality
- problematic school behaviour
- a history of economic hardship
- a chaotic household, and
- a significant separation from parent(s).

Similarly, Whitehouse (1985) also found that authors often looked for negative factors within families to indicate causes of offending. It is apparent then, that if the author has stereotypical attitudes and expectations of families, particularly around issues of 'race', gender and culture, s/he will tend to select factors which will confirm them. In so doing, reports may reflect the author's stereotypes and transmit them to the court thus re-inforcing any similar attitudes and beliefs held by the court.

In view of these perceptions, a second area of analysis was devised which would test for stereotypical use of those factors identified in reports as having caused offending to have taken place. This analysis was initially based on the factors identified by Harris and Webb (1987). However, it emerged that there were additional factors contained in the sample reports which were also included in the process of analysis. On this basis causative factors were identified in each report and comparisons made between reports prepared for defendants according to racial origin. Observations were then made about the potential impact of court reports which transmitted and reinforced racial stereotypes, especially in the context of results of the analysis of descriptive terms.

The overall effect of these analyses was to bring about some understanding of the potential nature and level of contribution court reports made to any discriminatory practice by report authors in the juvenile justice system and thus test out the third hypothesis of this study.

8   Quantitative research

In the first part of this chapter I shall build a profile all 282 cases which were heard in Wolverhampton Juvenile Court in 1990. The profile will take the form of an analysis of the age, gender, ethnicity and sentences imposed. In the first part of the chapter I shall demonstrate that African-caribbean defendants were over-represented in high-tariff sentences. In the second part I shall present analysis in the form of a comparison between ethnic groups in order to establish whether the over-representation amongst high-tariff sentences can be explained by seriousness or previous records.

The quantitative element of the study analysed profiles of 282 cases being all those heard in Wolverhampton Juvenile Court in 1990. It aims to identify general trends before revealing specific patterns in relation to high-tariff sentencing.

Age and Gender

With the exception of the number of fifteen year olds appearing in court in the year the number of defendants increased with age. The peak age of

Table 8.1
Comparison of the number of cases by age
(N=282)

Age	10	11	12	13	14	15	16	17	unknown	Total
No.	2	4	10	30	57	56	112	7	4	282
%	1	1	4	11	20	20	40	2	1	100

defendants was 16 years. 7.1% (n=20) of cases were girls and young women who were aged between 13 and 17 years. With the exception of the number of 15 year olds appearing in court the pattern of age is consistent with national trends. The relatively small number of 17 year olds represents those whose court proceedings commenced in the juvenile court when the defendant was still 16 but had reached their 17th birthday before sentence was imposed. The age of four defendants was unknown.

Ethnicity

Table 8.2 shows the ethnicity of children and young people in Wolverhampton (1991 census) as a means of comparison with the representation of the sample.

Table 8.2
Comparison of the ethnicity of the Wolverhampton population
aged 10-17 and the court sample

		White	*Asian*	*African-caribbean*	*Other*
Wolverhampton	*No.*	**17,407**	**5,685**	**1,269**	**333**
	%	**70**	**23**	**5**	**1**
Court sample	*No.*	**188**	**65**	**26**	**3**
	%	**67**	**9**	**23**	**1**

This comparison shows that whilst white defendants appeared in court in similar proportions to those in the population of this age group in Wolverhampton as a whole Asian defendants were under-represented in the court sample court and African-caribbean defendants were significantly over-represented. The ethnicity of defendants in the year of the study was very much in line with previous years as identified by Social Services Department monitoring reports. Consequently the over-representation of African-caribbean young people appearing before the court must be seen as a trend which begs the question why this should be. Furthermore it reinforces the need for research to understand the reasons for the imbalance and the importance of conducting this study.

Sentencing

Analysis of the sentences imposed in the 282 cases revealed that the whole range of disposal options were utilised by the court. Table 8.3 shows a comparison with sentencing in juvenile courts in England and Wales in 1989.

Table 8.3
Sentences imposed in Wolverhampton Juvenile Court in 1990:
a comparison with data for England and Wales, 1989

Disposal	Wolverhampton		England/Wales
	%	No.	%
Discharges	42	117	29
Compensation Order	2	6	2
Fine	11	30	20
Attendance Centre	16	44	15
Supervision Orders	12	32	19
s.7(7) Care Order	1	3	1
Community Service	6	16	5
Custodial Sentences	10	28	9
Deferred Sentence	2	6*	-

* Deferred sentences outstanding at 31 December 1990.

This comparison shows an above average use of discharges in and a less than average use of fines and Supervision Orders (with or without requirements). Other sentences imposed in Wolverhampton during the year are much in line with national trends. In broad terms this portrays that sentencing is largely in keeping with practice nationally. The greater use of discharges may be accounted for by the local economic circumstances. Demographic indicators traditionally place the town amongst the poorer areas in the country and for many years this has been reflected in the level of central government funding made available for social work services. The reasons for a lower than average use of Supervision Orders is less clear.

High tariff sentencing and 'race'

Reference has already been made to the over-representation of African-caribbean defendants appearing in court in comparison with the population of the age group in Wolverhampton. Further analysis of sentencing outcomes by 'race' revealed that whilst African-caribbean defendants were under-represented in relation to Supervision Orders imposed there was a significant over-representation where requirements were attached to Supervision Orders as well as in relation to Community Service Orders. Custodial sentences were imposed largely in line with the relative proportions of the court sample.

In relation to all high tariff sentences, i.e. Supervision, Community Service, Care Orders and custodial sentences, African-caribbean defendants were over-represented whilst there was an equivalent under-representation of white and Asian defendants. The inference that arises, therefore, is that whilst white and Asian defendants were more likely to have a low-tariff sentence imposed, African-caribbean defendants were more likely to receive a high tariff disposal.

Table 8.4
Comparisons of sample and high tariff disposals by 'race'

	White	African-caribbean	Asian
	%	%	%
Supervision Order	75	19	6
SO with reqs.	44	50	6
Community Service	37	56	6
Custodial sentences	70	25	7
All high tariff sents.	60	34	6
Court sample	67	23	9

At face value this would appear to suggest a possibility of disparity in sentencing. However, it is possible for this outcome to be explained by underlying features of the cases involved, i.e. seriousness off offending, antecedents, etc. In order to examine this possibility it is necessary to consider the material facts of the cases and make comparisons between 'race' groups.

Consideration was given to the utilisation of matched pairs as a process of comparison between defendants of different racial origin. It was decided, however, not to use this method in this study, first because of the limitations in the size of the sample in producing pairs with sufficiently matched features but also because of an inherent difficulty in determining variables outside the material facts of the case which could not be matched within the scope of this study. In circumstances where disparity of sentencing exists, are black defendants penalised for offending against white victims or simply by virtue of their 'blackness'. Mahoney (1991) argues that 'pairing' as a technique has limited effectiveness. Instead, comparisons are made between 'race' groups in a systematic manner to determine whether the characteristics of offending explain the apparent disparity noted above.

Seriousness of offending

One of the key elements in sentencing relates to the seriousness of the offence(s). The range of offences committed by white and African-caribbean defendants shows a large degree of similarity and whilst seriousness may vary within a single offence type it is reasonable to draw inferences from the similarity in the range offences committed, in overall terms the level of seriousness of offending between 'race' groups is also similar.

Such differences that occurred in the range of sentencing are characterised by charges of indecent assault and arson were only faced by white defendants whilst those of possession of an offensive weapon and soliciting were faced only by Black (African-caribbean and Asian) defendants. The main distinguishing features of the profiles of Black and white offending relate to the differing concentration on certain key offence types. Nearly a third of whites were charged with thefts of motor vehicles with a similar proportion having committed burglaries. Conversely, a quarter of Black defendants committed offences of robbery.

It is noticeable that the most serious charges faced by nearly 30% of African-caribbean defendants were in the lower range of offending; a band ranging from soliciting to theft. This compares with 13% of whites. At the other end of the scale, 30% of Blacks committed offences in the range of the four most serious offence types compared with 15% of whites. The cententration of offences committed by white defendants was in the middle of the band whilst the distribution of offending by African-caribbean defendants was more evenly spread across the whole of the range.

There are clearly difficulties in establishing seriousness on the basis of offence type alone because of the hidden detail relating to the aggravating factors relating to each case. Nevertheless, within the information available there is nothing to indicate any significant difference in the seriousness of offending revealed by each 'race' group. It is apparent, therefore, that sentencing differentials and the over-representation of African-caribbean defendants cannot be explained by the seriousness of offending.

Table 8.5
Comparison of offences by 'race'
(n=79)

	white	African-caribbean	Asian
	%	%	%
s.18 Wounding	2	3	-
Indecent Assault	6	-	-
Robbery	4	26	-
Arson	2	-	-
s.20/s.47 Assault	9	15	-
Theft of vehicle	32	7	20
Burglary	32	19	60
Theft	6	15	-
Receiving stolen goods	2	4	-
Poss'n of offensive weapon	-	4	-
Motoring Offences	4	4	-
Soliciting	-	4	20

Number of offences committed

In addition to the type of offences committed, another contributor to seriousness and hence sentencing is that of the number of offences committed. A second test was undertaken, therefore, to establish whether the

Table 8.6
Number of charges by 'race'
(n=79)

Number of charges	White	African-caribbean	Asian
	%	%	%
1-3	36	41	60
4-6	26	30	40
7-9	9	15	-
10-12	15	7	-
13-15	6	7	-
16-21	8	-	-

over-representation of African-caribbean defendants amongst high tariff sentences could be explained by a greater number of offences committed.

Table 8.6 shows that over 85% of African-caribbean defendants faced nine charges or fewer compared with 70% of white defendants. Conversely, less than 15% of African-caribbean defendants faced ten charges or more; the proportion of white defendants was 30%. It is apparent therefore, that, as with offence types, the disparity of sentencing of African-caribbean defendants cannot be explained by the number of offences committed.

Offences to be taken into consideration

In addition to the number and nature of offences with which the defendant is charged the sentencing outcome may also be affected by any other offences which the defendant asks the court to 'take into consideration' (tics). Whilst the nature and number of tics should not, of themselves, contribute to the severity of the penalty, they may be regarded as indicative of a lack of good character. Consequently, tics may have the effect of reducing any diminution in the severity of the sentence that is imposed especially if these offences were committed whilst the defendant was on bail.

It is often recognised that, at the time of a court hearing, defendants may have committed further offences that have gone undetected. It is the practice of certain solicitors to advise their clients to ask for other, undetected, offences to be taken into consideration in the context of the current hearing as a means of avoiding re-arrest. Similarly, it is the practice of some police forces to ask defendants if they have other offences they wish to have taken into consideration as a means of 'clearing up' otherwise unsolved crimes. Nevertheless tics are variables which are rarely included in studies of this sort despite the impact it may have on sentencing outcomes.

Further analysis was undertaken, then, to establish whether the over-representation of African-caribbean defendants could be explained by higher levels of offences to be taken into consideration. Table 8.7 shows that in almost three-quarters of African-caribbean defendants had no tics compared with 60% of whites. Only 8% of African-caribbean defendants had more than five tics whilst 23% of white defendants asked for offences numbering between five and 72 to be taken into consideration. All Asian defendants had five or fewer tics.

Clearly the number of tics cannot be regarded as an objective measure of criminal activity. Some defendants may have been encouraged to ask for offences to be taken into consideration whilst others may not have been. The accuracy of the number of offences identified by defendants may be open to question as may their motivation. It has been known for some defendants to decline to identify such offences in the knowledge that they have committed them whilst others have asked for offences to be taken into consideration

Table 8.7
Analysis of tics
(n=79)

Number of tics	white	African-caribbean	Asian
	%	%	%
0	60	74	60
1-5	17	19	40
6-10	9	-	-
11-15	2	4	-
16-20	6	-	-
21-25	-	4	-
26+	6	-	-

which they did not commit. The objectivity of the measure is not at stake here. Each defendant will have been sentenced with regard to the number of tics they have declared. From this data it is apparent that the over-representation of African-caribbean defendants cannot be explained by the number of offences the court were asked to take into account in sentencing.

Remand status

It is possible to gain an impression of the court's initial assessment of seriousness through the type of remand imposed. Although the seriousness of the offence is only one factor which determines the type of remand it remains a key indicator. Essentially it may be anticipated that the least serious offences will result in a remand on bail whilst for those which present as most serious the court have powers -dependant upon age- to remand to the care of the local authority or, ultimately, to custody.

Although other factors, including homelessness, would feature in such decisions, remand status was - at the time of the study - and remains indicative of the perceived likelihood of the commission of further offences. Analysis of the remand status of defendants gives further indication about the level of seriousness which the court attaches to the offence(s).

Table 8.8
Remand status
(n=79)

Remand type	white	African-caribbean	Asian
	%	%	%
Unconditional bail	28	63	80
Conditional bail	19	7	-
Remand to LA care	30	15	20
Remand in custody	23	15	-

Table 8.8 shows that whilst 63% of African-caribbeans and 80% of Asian defendants were unconditionally bailed only 28% of white defendants were similarly remanded. Even accounting for the inclination for courts to remand African-caribbean defendants in care on 'welfare' grounds these findings are significant in the extent to which they demonstrate that refusal of bail occurred most often in cases involving white defendants. Although there may be a variety of reasons for the refusal of bail it is apparent that the circumstances of offending by Black defendants was regarded by the courts as being of less concern than that by whites. In these circumstances it is apparent that the over-representation of African-caribbean defendants amongst high-tariff sentences cannot be explained by the level of seriousness of offending as represented by the number or nature of the current substantive charges, or as indicated by the offences to be taken into consideration or the remand status of the defendant.

Previous proceedings

Having observed that there is no discernible explanation for the over-representation of African-caribbean defendants amongst high tariff sentences arising from the seriousness of offending of the sample, it is necessary to look elsewhere for an explanation. A possible source of disparity may be differences in the previous criminal records evident between ethnic groups especially if the sample of African-caribbean defendants show signs of increased previous criminal activity.

It has already been noted that the operation of a tariff was such in 1990, that the severity of sentencing generally increased with each successive court appearance. The greater the number of court appearances increased the risk of the imposition of a high tariff sentence. As a result the, the sentence imposed in relation to the current offence(s) would, in addition to the seriousness, be influenced by the previous sentences that had been imposed on the defendant.

Table 8.9
Previous proceedings
(n=79)

Previous proceedings	white	African-caribbean	Asian
	%	%	%
1-3	20	33	60
4-6	6	33	20
7-9	45	19	20
10-12	6	11	-
13+	23	4	-

In order to test for differences in previous offending between ethnic groups, an analysis of the number of previous proceedings was undertaken. All defendants who were given high tariff sentences in the year had previous proceedings taken against them.

Table 8.9 shows that whilst two-thirds of African-caribbean defendants had up to six previous proceedings, nearly three-quarters (74%) of white defendants had seven or more; the highest concentration (45%) coming in the 7-9 band. Significantly, 23% of white defendants had 13 or more previous proceedings; over six times greater than the proportion of Black defendants in the corresponding band. One white defendant had 21 previous proceedings.

With such an overwhelming difference in the number of previous proceedings between the white and African-caribbean groups it becomes apparent that the over-representation of African-caribbeans amongst high tariff sentences cannot be explained by previous proceedings. Indeed, it is apparent that Black defendants had high tariff sentences imposed on them in circumstances where then number of previous proceedings was significantly lower than whites. However, the number of proceedings, alone, may not be an indication of the cumulative effect of previous offending as a whole. Clearly, a defendant who has appeared in court many times charged with a relatively small number of minor offences would not expect to have progressed through the tariff as rapidly as somebody charged with a greater number of more serious offences. Further examination is required of previous charges.

Previous charges

On examination the number of previous charges (Table 8.10) largely mirrors the analysis of previous proceedings; ranging in number from one to 28. Within the sample as a whole, the greater number of defendants were to be found at the lower end of the range. In general, the number of defendants decreased in proportion to the number of previous proceedings. However, there was one notable exception. The number of defendants in the 13-15 range of previous charges was significantly larger; second only to the two lowest ranges. However, this coincides with a corresponding 'bulge' in the analysis of previous proceedings, albeit less pronounced. In the case of one defendant, the number of previous charges was unknown.

Table 8.10
Comparison of number of previous charges by 'race'
(n=78)

Previous charges	White	African-caribbean	Asian
	%	%	%
1-3	19	26	20
4-6	21	19	40
7-9	13	22	40
10-12	6	15	-
13-15	26	15	-
16-18	4	4	-
19+	9	-	-

Analysis of the number of previous charges for each ethnic group revealed similar disproportion that was apparent with previous proceedings. Table 8.10 shows that over a quarter (26%) of the white group had between 13 and 15 previous charges. It also shows a significant difference in the distribution of defendants throughout the range of previous offending between ethnic groups. 53% of white defendants had nine or fewer previous charges compared with 67% of African-caribbeans. The large proportion of white defendants with between 13-15 previous charges contributed to the overall level (37%) who had 13 or more, almost double the percentage

(19%) of African-caribbean defendants with a similar previous record. It is apparent, then, that the over-representation of African-caribbean defendants is unexplained by the record of previous offending.

The age of high tariff offenders

Defendants upon whom high tariff sentences were imposed were chiefly in the 14-16 age band, although there were a small number (5) of younger defendants and one seventeen year old. This is in keeping with national trends and reflects the policy of the social services department and probation service of recommending the least intrusive sentencing option proportionate to the seriousness of the offence. Defendants under the age of 14 do not 'qualify' for a custodial sentence and, since high tariff sentences are generally regarded as alternatives to custody, there is a disinclination to make such recommendations in cases involving under 14s. Instead, where reports were provided, recommendations for under 14s would ordinarily favour fines and discharges.

Table 8.11
Age of the high tariff sentence group
(n=79)

Age	white	African-caribbean	Asian
	%	%	%
12	2	-	-
13	6	4	-
14	21	30	40
15	15	7	20
16	55	59	20
17	-	-	20

The age distribution of the high tariff sentence group largely reflected the trend in the overall court sample, although there were certain specific variations. Of particular note was the small number of 15 year olds. As noted earlier, the number of 15 year olds in the court sample was smaller than might have been anticipated given the general trend that numbers increase with age. In the court sample, the number of 15 year olds was similar in proportion to 14 year olds and approximately half the proportion of those aged 16. In the high tariff sentence group, however, the proportion

124

of 15 year olds was half that of 14 year olds and less than a quarter of those aged 16. This finding was rather surprising given the extended range of tariff options available at that time for 15 year olds. It was anticipated that the number of 14 year olds would be smaller and the number of 15 year olds might be larger, especially in view of the presumption that criminal activity increases with age. No explanation is suggested by the study for this curiosity.

When the group is analysed by ethnicity the relative absence of 15 year olds become even more pronounced. Table 8.11 shows that only 7% of African-caribbeans were 15 at the point of sentence compared with 15% of whites. With this exception, the trend is that African-caribbeans are marginally older as a group than whites and that the Asian group is older than both the other two.

These findings suggest that whites are developing more extensive criminal careers by an earlier age than Black defendants. In those circumstances, the sentencing response might have been expected to be more severe for white defendants. Certainly age, as a factor, did not explain the over-representation of African-caribbean defendants amongst high tariff sentences.

Since the over-representation of African-caribbean defendants amongst high tariff sentences is not explained by differences in the seriousness of offending, previous criminal activity or age it is necessary to consider other factors, e.g. recommendations by SIR authors.

SIR recommendations

Analysis of SIR recommendations in the cases which resulted in high tariff sentences being imposed showed that a wide range of sentencing alternatives were offered. All major tariff sentences were represented from conditional discharges at the lower end of the tariff to overt recommendations for custodial sentences at the other (irrespective of the existence of policies of the non-recommendation of custodial sentences in both SIR producing agencies). No clear recommendation was made in 14% of cases overall including two cases involving two Asian defendants. This option is used periodically by SIR authors who, being unable to recommend alternatives to custody, implicitly invite the imposition of a custodial sentence without directly breaching agency policy. In circumstances where all reports are scrutinised by an effective gate-keeping mechanism, no report with a recommendation of custody should find its way to court and there should be very few occasions when it is no possible to offer a viable alternative to custody package.

Low tariff disposals, i.e. discharges, fines or attendance centre orders, were recommended in one in five cases where high tariff sentences were imposed. The study does not suggest whether this is a reflection of overly optimistic or mis-targeted recommendations. As noted in chapter 4, the targeting of recommendations can be a hazardous exercise and can be undermined through the inclusion of additional charges or unforeseen tics at the last minute.

The operation of, or access to, gate-keeping panels should reduce the risk of mis-targeting recommendations but it is incumbent upon SIR authors following laid down procedures as much as it is a matter of ensuring that the procedures facilitate the short timescales that are frequently a factor in court report preparation. Practice has shown that procedures are not universally followed. SIRs were frequently submitted to the court without reference to any gate-keeping or supervisory process.

Analysis of SIR recommendations by ethnic group produce some notable differences in practice (Table 8.12). First, whilst supervision orders (without additional requirements) were recommended in 21% of cases involving white defendants, there were no similar recommendations in cases involving African-caribbean defendants. Secondly, one-third of all African-caribbean defendants had a recommendation of a supervision order with a specified activity requirement. Thirdly 26% of all African-caribbean defendants had community service orders recommended.

The combination of these factors reveals an unwillingness to recommend supervision orders and an over willingness to recommend alternative to custody measures especially in cases involving Black defendants. This seems to reinforce my earlier observation that SIR authors were predisposed to making alternative to custody recommendations in cases involving Black defendants out of concern for the increased risk of custody. In such circumstances, Magistrates are invited to impose community alternatives in cases where the seriousness of the offence(s), the previous criminal record and age of Black defendants would suggest were unwarranted and where a supervision order might be more appropriately recommended. In effect, the recommendation is not addressing the material facts of these cases but trying, in advance, to address the Magistrates' response to the defendant.

It would appear, then, that whilst the over-representation of African-caribbeans cannot be explained by the seriousness of their offences and the extent of their previous criminal records, the over-representation can be explained, in part, by a combination of the absence of recommendations in SIR and by inappropriate recommendations in cases involving Black defendants.

126

Table 8.12
SIR recommendations
(n=79)

Recommendation	white	African-caribbean	Asian
	%	%	%
Cond. discharge	2	4	-
Fine	2	4	-
Attendance centre order	9	19	40
Supervision order	21	-	20
S. O. with I. T. req.	2	4	-
S.O. with Spec. Act.	19	33	-
Community service	23	26	-
Deferred sentence	4	-	-
Custodial sentence	2	-	-
No recommendation	13	11	40

Summary of findings

The study involved analysis of a sample which, although small, represented all cases heard in Wolverhampton Juvenile Court in 1990. In overall terms, African-caribbean defendants would appear to be treated differently in the local justice system and this differential treatment would not appear to be explained by the material facts of the cases. 'Race, therefore, would appear to be an important determinant in its own right suggesting that discriminatory processes are at work. The differential treatment of African-caribbean defendants was manifest in the following ways:

1. In comparison with the ethnic composition of the population of 10 - 17 year olds in Wolverhampton, African-caribbeans were over-represented in the court sample whilst whites and Asians were under-represented. This study offers no explanation for this finding which must continue to be a matter of some concern to the local community and consequently should be the subject of further research to begin to understand the processes which cause this phenomenon.

2. In overall terms, African-caribbean defendants were over-represented amongst high tariff sentences. Specifically, African-caribbean defendants were given more direct alternative to custody sentences -

127

specified activity and community service orders - but were given fewer supervision orders.

3. Whilst there were some differences in the characteristics of offending between ethnic groups the overall seriousness of offending was regarded as similar for both white and African-caribbean groups.

4. The number of charges faced by African-caribbean defendants was substantially lower than the number faced by whites.

5. Similarly, the number of offences which Black defendants asked the court to take into consideration was substantially lower than for whites.

6. White defendants were much more likely to be remanded into the care of the local authority or into custody than Black defendants.

7. African-caribbean defendants given high tariff sentences had significantly fewer previous proceedings than whites.

8. Similarly, those lower levels of previous proceedings were reflected in proportionately lower numbers of previous charges faced by Black defendants than whites.

9. Consequently, the over-representation of African-caribbean defendants amongst high tariff sentences could not be explained by the material facts of the cases - the seriousness of offending or previous criminal records.

10. No recommendations were made during the year of supervision orders where the subject of the report was African-caribbean. Conversely, African-caribbean defendants were more likely than whites to have recommendations made for specified activity requirements or community service orders - direct alternative to custody measures.

These findings suggest that social work and probation service system intervention was not overcoming disadvantage for Black defendants. On the contrary, it is apparent that SIR practice in relation to recommendations compounded disadvantage, especially in cases involving African-caribbean defendants. However, recommendations constitute only one element of SIRs. As an instrument intended to influence sentencing, it is necessary to examine the content of SIRs in order to identify whether Black defendants were further disadvantaged by the way in which they were portrayed. It is this factor which is addressed in the next chapter.

9   Qualitative research

Reference has already been made to the fact that although evidence suggests that there is disparity of sentencing according to ethnicity, a simple analysis of court sentencing does not establish where responsibility for that disparity lies. Neither does it identify what areas of practice need to be improved to avoid discriminatory processes. There has been an implicit assumption that if there is disparity, then, responsibility for that lies initially with the police because of the crucial role in arresting and charging, etc. or with Magistrates in connection with the sentencing role. However, since sentencers enter towards the end of a process during which decisions have been made and interpretations placed on the facts of the matter by other agencies and individuals, it is unsafe as well as unjust to assume that responsibility is theirs alone. Some effort must be made to untangle the various influences of the various actors in the system in order to isolate what effect each contribution has on the whole sentencing process.

In that context it is the purpose of this study, having first established whether there is any apparent discriminatory sentencing pattern, to examine social work practice to establish what contribution is made to discriminatory processes. In order to do that attention was focused on SIRs which, in 1990, formed the basis of social work input into the court and sentencing processes.

There followed, therefore, a qualitative analysis of SIR content in order to examine whether there were different messages being conveyed to sentencers about defendants according to the ethnicity of the defendant. Examination of previous SIR content analysis studies revealed that invariably the analysis was undertaken or framed by researcher connected, to a greater or lesser degree with the social work profession. The model most frequently employed seemed to be that of studying SIRs and forming an impressionistic assessment of the content and tone of the reports (see, for example, Whitehouse, 1986; Pimm and Lines, 1987). However, it was apparent that there was a need to design and undertake the analysis in a way which revealed how messages communicated in SIRs were being received by sentencers in order to gain some insight into how sentencing decision making was being influenced.

Methodology

In order to address the issue of the way information in SIRs was received a two-pronged system of analysis was designed: the first to concentrate on the language used by SIR authors to describe the characteristics of the defendant and the second related to causal factors of offending identified by authors. In this way SIRs would be assessed for the choice and use of language as well as the perceptions of each author about the factors that had precipitated the offence(s).

The qualitative analysis was based on a sample of 123 SIRs drawn from the total of 186 reports that were presented to the court during the year (1990) representing 66% of all reports prepared. From this sample, 364 words and phrases were extracted which had been used to describe the characteristics of the defendants. These descriptive terms were collated into a score sheet which was sent to Magistrates who were asked to mark, on a five point grid, a point corresponding to the positive or negative image that they perceived for each term. To eliminate built in bias to responses, no values were ascribed to the grid aside from a model continuum demonstrating the poles as 'favourable' and 'unfavourable'. For similar reasons, each document was assembled in different page order to avoid the possibility of response fatigue. For this reason, pages were given an identifying letter instead of numbers.

A total of 145 questionnaires were mailed to Magistrates who, at the time, sat on Juvenile Benches in three Petty Sessional Divisions (PSDs) in England. Of these, 64 (44%) were completed and returned. In speaking of mail surveys, Moser and Kalton (1971, p. 262) note: 'strenuous efforts ...[are] needed to bring the response rate above 30% or 40%'. Against this benchmark the response rate of 44% from Magistrates to a mail survey of twelve pages was very satisfactory and gave a sound base from which to analyse SIRs.

The Magistrates were drawn from three PSDs selected as a representative sample. Magistrates in Wolverhampton were not surveyed in order to avoid any risk of appearing to influence local decision making and sentencing.

Instead, three other PSDs were identified and their co-operation was elicited via the Clerk to the Justices in each PSD. The first PSD is located in a midland shire county, the second is in a former county borough in the south-east of England and the third is a city in the West Midland conurbation.

Copies of the survey document were distributed to the Clerk to the Justices in each PSD to be forwarded to each Magistrate who responded anonymously; returning the completed in a self-addressed envelope coded to identify the PSD. Respondents received instructions on how to complete the score sheet and were invited to make any additional comments alongside each descriptive term. They were asked to record their immediate responses to each term and informed that the whole exercise should not take any longer than 30 minutes. In this way, it was hoped to gain responses based upon instantaneous reactions in much the same way that might occur in the courtroom.

Upon receipt of each completed questionnaire values were ascribed to the points on the grid. A value of one was given to the most negative ('unfavourable') point on the grid progressing through the range to a value of five for the most positive ('favourable') point. A deadline had been set for responses following which, completed score sheets from each PSD were gathered together and total scores calculated for each bench to produce a 'bench mark' for each descriptive term. As there were a different number of returned score sheets from each bench, the 'bench mark' was divided by the number of responses to provide a 'base score' for comparison between PSDs. In most cases, the variation between 'base scores' was within 0.5 for each descriptive term. The widest margin of difference was 0.9 which occurred on just nine occasions. The 'base scores' for each term were added together and divided by three (the number of PSDs) in order to give a 'mean score' which could then be used for the SIR analysis.

A total score was calculated for each SIR by adding together the mean scores of each of the descriptive terms used and dividing by the number of terms. Thus each SIR received a score of between 1.00 and 5.00, calculated to two decimal places reflecting the negativity or positivity of the image communicated by the report. Following initial analysis to develop a profile of the sample, a second analysis was undertaken to compare the scores on the basis of the ethnicity of the defendants to establish whether any group was portrayed more positively than another.

First, general observations were made on the basis of the additional comments made by Magistrates. Of the total respondents, 35 (54.7%) made additional responses which broadly related to three main themes. First, terms which described physical characteristics, for example, tall, short, thin, etc.

were considered to be superfluous and unnecessary to the sentence decision making process. Secondly, statements of opinion relating to, for example, improved behaviour, were considered to be inadequate alone without corroborating evidence. Thirdly, Magistrates took the opportunity to register concern in relation to certain descriptive terms which were regarded as unprofessional, subjective and/or stereotypical. In one case, a defendant was described as being 'like a wild animal' whilst in another a defendant was described as 'an attractive girl'. Both terms attracted criticisms from Magistrates who stated that such observations would cast doubt on the validity of the report before them and upon future reports written by the same author.

The number of descriptive terms used in SIRs

In building a profile of all reports in the sample, first, a note was made of the number of descriptive terms used which ranged from none in nine reports to 17 descriptive terms in one report (Table 9.1). In one case where

Table 9.1
The number of descriptive terms used in SIRs
(n=123)

No. of terms used	No. of reports	%
0	9*	7
1-2	17	14
3-5	49	40
6-8	28	23
9-10	12	10
11+	8	7

* Includes one report where access to the defendant was denied.

there was no description of the defendant apparent in the report it was established that the subject's guardian had denied access by the social worker. That eight other reports were bereft of any description of the defendants seems contrary to the purpose and function of SIRs. A report that contains no description can barely be deemed to have placed the offence and the offender in context.

In most cases where two descriptive terms were used they were employed cumulatively. That is to say, either both terms were positive (i.e. scored more than 3.00) or they were both negative (i.e. scored less than 3.00). Rarely was one positive and one negative descriptive term used in the same report.

Overall, where fewer descriptive terms were used, the impression of the defendant that was communicated was vague and it is questionable whether anything other than the merest hint of the subject was conveyed. The greatest number of reports were those which contained three descriptive terms (21%).

Descriptive terms and balanced reports

The reports were then analysed for the range of scores in relation to the number of descriptive terms used. The lowest score was 2.1; the highest was 4.0. Table 2.2 shows that the widest range of scores were found where fewer descriptive terms were used. Largely, reports increased in balance in proportion to the number of descriptive terms used. That is to say, the more complete portrayals of defendants were also the more balanced. There were three reports employing more than five descriptive terms where the image portrayed by each term was negative. It is not possible to quantify the cumulative effect this might have but it can be anticipated that those reports would be perceived as most damning of their subjects and could hardly be regarded as presenting a 'balanced' picture of the individuals.

It is important always, not to confuse quality with quantity. That a report contained more description does not imply that the description was more comprehensive or more positive. Neither does it presume greater effectiveness and influence with the court.

The individual scores for each report were plotted on a graph in relation to the number of descriptive terms used and average and median scores were calculated. In just three out of eleven cases the average scores were of a value less than 3.00, whilst only two median scores were below 3.00. This suggests that overall, reports tended to be framed positively.

For the purpose of classification, the reports were divided into three groups. Using a score of 3.00 as the axis, reports which scored 3.32 or more were defined as positive in overall tone. Those which scored 2.68 or less were defined as negative and those in the middle range of scores (2.68 to 3.32) were classified as conveying a neutral image.

Of the overall sample, excluding the nine reports where no descriptive terms were used, 21 reports (18%) fell into the negative zone whilst 38 SIRs

(33%) were classified as positive. The majority of reports (49%) achieved scores in the middle band and were defined as neutral or 'balanced' in the language used to describe the defendant.

Figure 9.1 shows the relative balance in reports according to the number of descriptive terms used. It confirms that in relation to positivity and negativity, the proportion of neutral or 'balanced' reports increases with the number of terms. Notice how the centre column in each range becomes

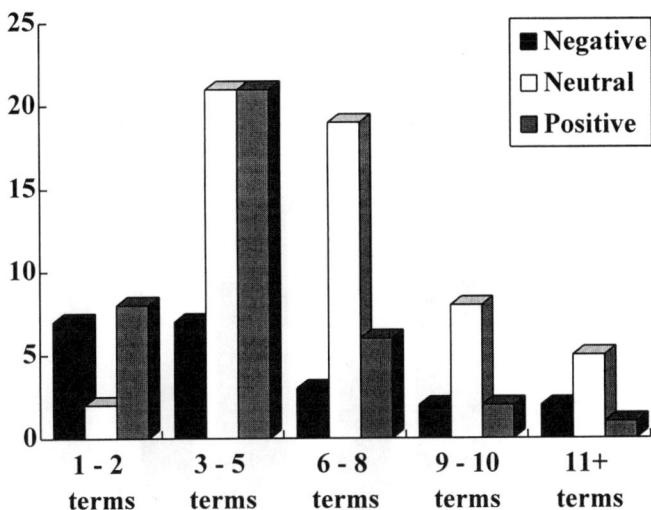

Figure 9.1   Descriptive terms and balance in SIRs

more prominent as the number of terms used increases. Notice also that the columns representing positivity is equal to, or greater in each case than negative values, with the exception of those reports where eleven or more terms were used. It is apparent from these findings that, in overall terms, reports were largely 'balanced' in their representation of defendants in that the majority of reports (49%) were classified as neutral according to the images perceived by Magistrates in the descriptive terms used. Where reports were not neutral, authors tended to err towards positivity in their portrayals of defendants. However, establishing the balance of the reports according to the images portrayed through the language used to describe defendants does not infer that the reports were objective portrayals of the defendants, only that the manner they were portrayed was balanced.

'Race' and SIR content

Having completed an analysis of the number and nature of descriptive terms in SIRs overall, analysis of the reports was then undertaken with regard to the ethnicity of defendants. Whilst there were broad similarities between the groups it was noted that the widest range in scores from the most negative to the most positive occurred in the white group. The lowest score for a report on a white defendant was 0.2 below any other report. The narrowest band was that relating to Asian defendants where the lowest score was 2.29 and the highest was 3.80.

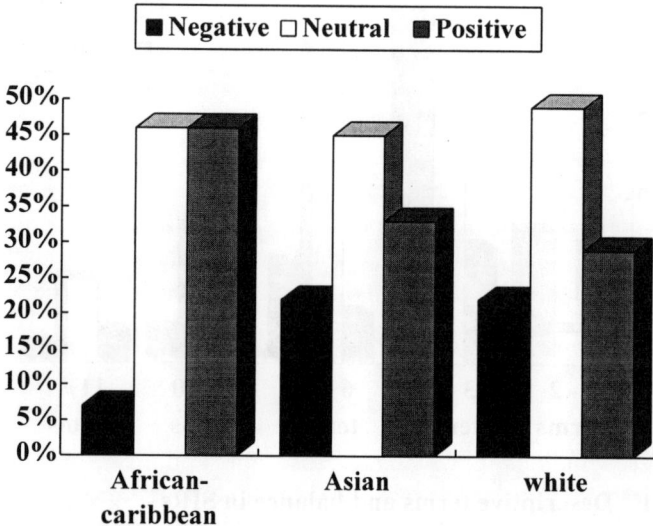

Figure 9.2   Ethnicity and balanced reports

Average scores for all reports were above the median in each group although the margin was smaller for white defendants than Blacks. This suggested that reports tended to be positive overall and particularly so for Black defendants.

Figure 9.2 shows the similarity in distribution of reports for Asian and white defendants and how a low percentage of negative reports is mirrored by a higher percentage of positive reports. Neutrality in SIRs was relatively even across all three groups. Of particular note is the low percentage of negative reports prepared for African-caribbean defendants and a correspondingly higher level of positive reports. Whilst negative reports were prepared for two in every ten Asian or white defendants the proportion of negative reports for African-caribbean defendants was less than one in ten. On this basis, the disparity of sentencing identified in the quantitative study would appear to have some other cause than negative report writing. On the contrary, positive reports were produced as frequently as neutral reports for African-caribbean defendants (46%). Asian (33%) and white (29%) defendants were less likely to be the subject of positive reports.

In view of these findings greater confidence in SIR practice began to emerge. In particular, it seemed that discriminatory practice was less evident in relation to reports written in relation to African-caribbean defendants than might have been expected. One can only speculate that high levels of positivity and low levels of negativity in reports have similar origins in motivation to the drive to make more community alternative recommendations for African-caribbean defendants. That is to say, perhaps social workers feel the need to be more positive in relation to African-caribbean defendants because of their perceptions that there is a greater degree of risk of custody in these cases. Alternatively, the high proportion of positive reports may also reflect what is shown through the quantitative analysis, namely, that there is less to be negative about because African-caribbean defendants had committed fewer, less serious offences and were less criminally active than their white counterparts.

Consistent SIR practice

Whilst these findings gave some cause for optimism, observation of individual reports gave some cause for concern about consistency in social work practice. There were examples in which it was clear that there had been inadequate attention to detail. Discrepancies became particularly apparent when comparing reports produced in those circumstances where defendants appeared in court more than once in the study period. A typical example was of a white, male defendant who, on his first court appearance was described in the SIR as 'tall', was described by the same author later the same year as 'short'. Even allowing for a reduced growth rate, it is unlikely that the subject might be regarded as 'tall for his age' and 'short for his age' within 12 months. This example also exposes the folly of including superfluous material. There are many ways for court report authors to 'shoot themselves in the foot' with accidental inaccuracies without doing so with information which is unlikely to be material to the case.

The overwhelming majority of cases involving multiple court appearances in the year showed high levels of consistency. Perry (1974) expressed concerns about the frequency with which authors replicated previous reports; updating them to take account of the current case. Such replication was apparent only once in the sample of SIRs analysed.

There were examples where the use of language seemed rather subjective, if not, on occasions, emotive. Reference has already been made to the report which described a defendant as 'like a wild animal'. Other terminology was sometimes vague or jargonistic and communicated little of value. Of note here was the frequency which social science terminology was used with little to quantify or reinforce what was otherwise a bland assertion. Phrases like, 'low' or 'poor self esteem' were rarely substantiated by examples of behaviour or other evidence which caused the author to come to that view.

Observations about defendants' 'race' or ethnicity were rarely made and the practice of the 1970s and 1980s to identify the religious persuasion or the date when Black families migrated to the area were, thankfully, absent. One defendant was described as being 'of mixed race' but there was no elaboration on the relevance of this fact to the circumstances of the case. Neither were any apparent enquiries made into the effects of racism experienced by Black defendants. Indeed, in overall terms, the ethnicity of most defendants was not apparent from the content of reports. Matters of 'race', ethnicity and experiences of racism, it seems, were matters to be avoided in SIRs.

However, whilst it has been noted that reports overall conveyed largely neutral or positive images of defendants; especially those written in relation to African-caribbean defendants, descriptions of defendants represent only one facet of the way information is communicated. Harris and Webb (1987), in their work focusing on the disproportionate power relationship between supervisors and supervisees, identified nine 'problem' areas which were frequently perceived by supervisors as the causes of offending. This represents another important facet of court report practice; namely, the framing and defining of those circumstances which are regarded by social workers as the causes of offending and the manner in which offenders are consequently pathologised.

Problems and causes of offending

Following the classifications identified by Harris and Webb (1987) the reports were analysed for the causes they highlighted as explanations for the defendant's offending. The original classifications -

- disruption caused by separation

138

- significant separation from parent(s)

- a chaotic household

- problematic parental disciplining

- a history of economic hardship

- deviant family norms

- problematic school behaviour

- parental criminality

- absence from school

- were supplemented by three others: external influences, including peer group and environmental pressure; issues of health and abuse, including substance abuse and self harm, and other causes, being those that did not easily fall into any other classification.

Of the sample, 110 reports offered one or more explanations or causes of offending. A total of 354 causes were identified demonstrating that in many cases social workers perceived there to be a combination of factors at work. Significant separation from parent(s) and peer group pressure were the most commonly identified factors, featuring in 1 in 7 of the reports. The second group of causes that were identified were absence from school and problematic parental disciplining which featured in 1 in every 8 reports. Illness and/or self abuse featured in 1 in 11 reports whilst deviant family norms and problematic school behaviour were highlighted as causes of offending in 1 in 12 reports.

Analysis of the reports on the basis of the ethnicity of the defendant revealed some interesting similarities and differences. Problematic parental disciplining featured prominently in reports from all three ethnic groups as did peer group pressure. However, whilst problematic parental disciplining was distributed relatively evenly (31% - 44%) between the three groups, there were significant differences in the proportion of reports where peer group pressure was identified; featuring in 39% of reports relating to white defendants, 54% of African-caribbean defendants' reports and 78% of SIRs for Asian defendants.

Whilst the causes identified in reports were distributed widely across the classifications there were some notable exceptions. Significant separation from parents and absence from school featured highly with white and African-caribbean defendants but was much less prominent for Asian defendants. Over 53% of reports relating to white defendants highlighted significant separation as a cause of offending; more than double the frequency in SIRs relating to Asians and African-caribbeans. Conversely, a chaotic household was identified in 56% of reports on Asian defendants compared with 25% of SIRs on white subjects whilst it did not feature in any report produced in relation to African-caribbean defendants. Similarly, illness and/or self abuse arose in 44% of reports on Asian defendants and a third of reports on whites but less than 10% of those relating to African-caribbean defendants.

These findings pose two questions. The first question relates to the objectivity of social workers in making assessments of offending causation. The second question relates to the impact that issues of causation have on sentencing.

I have already noted that social work is steeped in the values of the dominant culture. As a consequence, social workers make assessments about individuals in relation to the extent to which they deviate from a range of accepted norms and values. Accepted, that is, by the social worker as an outcome of the interplay between personal and professional, individual and organisational models of 'normality'. It is against that model that defendants are assessed and the areas of life experience and personal circumstance which differ from that model become noteworthy; to be held up as significant. Assessment of causative factors, therefore, need not be an objective assessment based on firmly established principles but may be set against the shifting sand of personal attitudes and trends in social policy. The outcome of assessment is unlikely, therefore, to be measurably scientific. Indeed, two different social workers may produce very different assessments of the causes why the same person offended.

Different perspectives regarding the causes of offending may occur, then, because of differences in the personal value base of individual social workers. Equally they may occur because of differences in the social work perspective from which the worker operates. Additionally, there is an intrinsic assumption that we know why children and young people offend. And yet, it is apparent that notions of the causation of offending are fluid. Witness the changes in perceptions between the Longford Report (1964), which identified that offending is the product of inequality in society, and the White Paper, 'Children in Trouble (1968) which contended that juvenile had no single cause.

In certain cases the causation link may be direct and may be confidently ascribed in a court report. A young person who is offending whilst being absent from school has an identifiable and addressable cause of offending. For the most part causes of offending may be rather more speculative than proven. This has an impact upon the second question arising from the findings. What effect does the identified causes of offending have upon sentencing?

Sheila Brown (1991) and Parker et al (1989) reveal how social background information is used capriciously to reinforce the social constructs of individual defendants developed by Magistrates. One of the functions of sentencing is to deter future offending. In circumstances whereby Magistrates observe that the same conditions are in place which led to the current offences being committed the importance of sentencing as a deterrent increases. If those conditions are speculative, vague and are built on stereotypical images the prospect of changing them and diminishing the perceived risk of re-offending is reduced. Consequently, a greater compulsion to utilise deterrent sentencing arises.

I previously made the observation that to be a lone parent at this time carries assumptions about parenting ability and the likelihood of children becoming offenders. Interestingly, this factor emerged prominently as an identified cause in the SIR content analysis under the heading of 'significant separation from parent(s)'. These assumptions occur without any substantive evidence. Nevertheless, lone parents experience the consequences of such prejudice daily and speak of their frustration at their children being labelled as a result of it. Similar stereotypes occur in relation to each of the causative labels which are identified. The effect of having that label ascribed to a child is that s/he will be dealt with prejudicially by all manner of people. When those stereotypical states, i.e. lone parenthood, problem school behaviour, deviant family norms, economic hardship, etc., are superimposed by 'race', the effect of that prejudice is even more profound. To many people, the concept of a lone parent is problematic; a lone Black parent is even more so. Consequently, causes of offending may reinforce stereotypical images which, by definition, are beyond the control of the individual to change. Since the individual cannot make the required change to bring about avoidance of offending in the future it encourages Magistrates to use another weapon in their armoury to reduce re-offending, namely, more punitive sentencing.

There is a sense in which, by identifying explanations for offending which are beyond the control of the individual defendant, court report authors are effectively saying to Magistrates, 'please be lenient, it wasn't her/his fault'. This view would appear to be reinforced by the frequency with which explanations or causes of offending are cited in reports. From a sample of 110 reports, 354 explanations were extracted; an average of over three per report. It is apparent, however, that if the message communicated is a plea for leniency, it becomes processed as circumstances which are not conducive to reduced offending. The inference from these findings, therefore, are that the backdrop against which defendants are set, as expressed in the form of causes of explanation rooted in social background information, risks perpetuating stereotypical images. The groups who are likely to be disadvantaged most by stereotyping are Black groups, not only because of endemic racism directly, but also because against all measures relating to housing, income, education, employment, etc. - all the issues which are deemed to create the environment for offending behaviour - Black people in Britain fare worse than whites (see, for example, Policy Studies Institute (1984)). Therefore, Black defendants are most likely to be disadvantaged in sentencing terms by the inclusion of non-specific explanations for offending which cannot be addressed by the individual.

The overall conclusion I would draw from the qualitative study was that it demonstrated that whilst Black defendants generally, and African-caribbean defendants in particular, were represented more positively as individual people, in court reports they were set against a back drop which was so potentially stereotypical that the positive individual image was undermined. Indeed, perversely, the fact that Black defendants were portrayed so positively could possibly have created greater motivation to 'rescue' them from the hopeless circumstances in which they live.

In overall terms, whilst it was found that African-caribbean defendants were over-represented amongst the juvenile court population and amongst those given high tariff sentences, that over-representation could not be explained by the material facts of the cases insofar as they were revealed through issues of seriousness of offending and previous record, etc. There appears to be some evidence of a propensity to make community alternative recommendations in relation to Black defendants in circumstances where those recommendations would not be made if the defendant was white. Furthermore, in relation to SIRs, although Black defendants were more likely to be portrayed in a positive light in terms of how they were described as individuals, they were likely to be set against stereotypical social background information which undermined that positive image.

In the final chapter I shall consider these findings, draw some conclusions and make recommendations to address the issues that have been identified.

10 Summary of findings and recommendations

The purpose of this study was to test out three hypotheses in relation to the operation of the juvenile justice system in Wolverhampton in 1990.

1. There is disparity of sentencing between ethnic groups.

2. This disparity is manifest in higher tariff sentencing of Black defendants in relation to whites.

3. Responsibility for this disparity is, in part, associated with SIR content.

Within the limitations of a case study based upon a sample of 282 cases heard in Wolverhampton Juvenile Court in 1990 it was found that African-caribbean defendants are over-represented and Asians are under-represented in the court population in relation to the ethnicity of the town's 10-17 year old population. It is also apparent that African-caribbean defendants were given disproportionately high tariff sentences in relation to white and Asian defendants. This disproportion could not be explained by the seriousness of the offences, the number of charges faced or previous records. Furthermore, it would appear that African-caribbean defendants may be accelerated through the tariff by the apparent reluctance to recommend supervision orders and the over-enthusiastic recommendation of alternative to custody measures. As a result of these findings it would seem that there is evidence to support the first two hypotheses.

With regard to the third hypothesis it was found that SIRs were generally framed more positively for Black defendants - particularly African-caribbean defendants - than for whites in terms of the language used to describe the individual defendants. However, it would appear that this positive framing was off-set by reference to stereotypical social background information which was perceived as causative of the offending.

Within months of the study being completed new legislation was introduced replacing social inquiry reports with pre-sentence reports (PSRs). The Criminal Justice Act 1991 requires courts to obtain and consider a PSR before forming an opinion about the suitability for an offender of a probation, community service, combination or supervision order. There is also an obligation to obtain and consider a PSR before determining whether or not custodial sentencing criteria are met or the length of a custodial sentence. These requirements were reinforced by 'National Standards' (Home Office, 1992, 1995) which provide a framework of guidance for the production of PSRs. The combined effect of the Act and the 'National Standards' was to make important changes to the purpose of court reports and consequently to the content of them. Most notably, authors were guided to analyse the current offence(s) and consider *relevant* information about the offender before drawing conclusions, including a proposal for the most suitable community sentence where relevant. In the context of 'relevant information about the offender', this was further defined as 'previous offending and response to supervision, motivation, strengths, personal problems...'. Consequently, scope for the free-ranging 'welfare' orientated SIR content was seriously curtailed in favour of information directly related to the current offence(s).

Theoretically, then, practice should have moved on. Some of the issues identified by this study should, coincidentally, have been addressed through the changed court report framework, especially in its most recently revised manifestation (Home Office, 1995). In drawing conclusions and making recommendations it is my intention to address the changed circumstances in which practice now takes place as well as highlighting issues which remain an on-going item on the (youth) justice agenda.

This study confirms what many local practitioners believed, namely. that Black young people - primarily African-Caribbeans - are over-represented in court and amongst those given high tariff sentences. It was apparent whilst conducting the study that authors had absorbed that belief to the point of actively taking steps to address the over-representation in their practice. Ironically, the strategies they had adopted appear to compound rather than diminish - not to speak of eliminate - the over-representation. There are, therefore, unintended consequences from practice which, far from resolving the issues, seem to exacerbate the discrimination experienced by Black African-caribbean defendants.

Two areas of social work practice have been revealed by this study which, although well intentioned, are counter-productive to the needs of Black defendants, namely;

a) the inclination to over-compensate for the risk of custody through alternative to custody recommendations at the expense of supervision orders and,

b) the inclusion of stereotypical social background information upon which the causes of offending are hung.

Since the implementation of the Criminal Justice Act 1991 it has been the practice in the courts to indicate what sentence band is being contemplated in relation to each defendant. The prospect of 'second guessing' therefore, has been much diminished. No longer should PSR authors be mis-targeting alternative to custody proposals. There is still scope however, for the assumption that Magistrates are contemplating sentencing at the upper end of the sentencing band in cases involving Black defendants. Similarly, in cases involving Black defendants where Magistrates indicate that they are contemplating a custodial sentence which would have the effect of leap-frogging a supervision order, a strong case should be made for a lower tariff sentence rather than an alternative to custody proposal. Proposals should be made on the strength of the material facts of each case; the ethnicity of the defendant should not determine the proposal to be made.

In relation to effective system management, gate-keeping panels should monitor local sentencing trends to ensure that Black defendants are not being accelerated through the tariff. PSR proposals should also be monitored in the light of the sentencing patterns to ensure that there is no collusion with discriminatory practice.

The practice of responding to the greater risk of Black defendants being given custodial sentences by presenting alternative to custody packages is a failed strategy of damage limitation. Such proposals are made from a position of professional weakness and as such are counter-productive since they reinforce the weak position both of social workers and Black defendants. A new and positive strategy is required which can address discriminatory practice from a position of strength.

In view of the widespread trend for Black defendants not to be given supervision orders there is a need for a comprehensive policy within each social services department to raise the profile of supervision as a sentencing option. A policy statement should be produced which would include details

146

of a programme in which Magistrates and social workers alike can have confidence that the needs and offending behaviour of Black defendants will be addressed. The programme should build on the framework of 'national standards' (Home Office, 1995) to incorporate positive measures for addressing offending behaviour in a creative and imaginative package. Supervision orders should not, like old soldiers, fade away, but should reach a negotiated conclusion. Progress on the part of defendants should be rewarded through early revocation of orders whilst those who fail to comply should be dealt with in accordance with 'national standards'.

It is apparent that Magistrates rarely see evidence of successful intervention. Supervision orders which are not breached often drift until they have elapsed. It is important for defendants, social workers and Magistrates that successful orders are concluded in the same arena in which they began; in court. In addition, social services departments should give regular feedback to courts about the successes of supervision. Annual reports which present an overview of local supervision order activity and re-offending rates in relation to other disposals could do much to paint a positive image of a proactive sentencing option.

In a climate where the 'prison works' message is widely broadcast it is important that supervision is 'marketed' as a positive and successful alternative within the local community. This includes making information available to the local press and radio both in relation to the success of the overall programme as well as individual programmes - so far as confidentiality allows. The adage states 'nothing breeds success like success' and much success is brought about by positive framing. The packaging and marketing of supervision as a constructive response to youthful offending can do much to increase confidence in this sentencing option. When confidence levels in supervision increase social workers can make positive proposals in PSRs with a greater likelihood of their adoption by Magistrates. In this way positive supervision order proposals can replace the current defensive practice of early use of alternatives to custody.

Many social services departments are committed to system management and have adopted diversionary policies. The findings of this study would seem to validate that approach. However, it has also demonstrated that since 'race' is not a concious consideration within ideology Black young people will continue to be disadvantaged without positive action is taken to address discriminatory processes within the system.

The issue of stereotyping in reports is one that should have been addressed by the replacement of SIRs with a standardised PSR format. Dispensing with personal and social histories which so frequently comprised the substantive

147

part of SIRs and focusing instead on that material, prescribed by 'national standards', which directly relates to the commission of the offence(s) should have largely eliminated the source of much stereotypical material. However, it is apparent that practitioners have found space for the liberal inclusion of such material under the heading of 'relevant information about the offender' which was introduced in the first manifestation of the 'national standards' (Home Office, 1992). More worrying still, is the interpretation by some youth justice consultants that 'welfare' material, previously outlawed from PSRs, may now be included under the heading of 'risk assessment' - introduced as a PSR component in the revised 'national standards' (Home Office, 1995).

The exclusion of this type of material was unpopular with social workers and Magistrates alike. Social workers regretted the perceived loss of opportunity to engender compassion and sympathy for children and young people who were as much victims of circumstance as they were perpetrators of criminal activity. Magistrates regretted the absence of material upon which to build or confirm stereotypical judgements which justified more punitive sentencing measures. In order to avoid the capricious use of social background information in the determination of sentencing it is important that stereotypical material is excluded from reports. The alternative is that Black African-caribbean defendants will continue to be sentenced in a way which cannot be justified by the material facts of their offending. Only that information which is *directly* relevant to and forms a primary link with the circumstances in which offending took place should be included.

Part of the issue relates to a lack of awareness by a profession which is steeped in the dominant white culture and which is manifest in a lack of awareness amongst individual practitioners of their own racism, their own value base and of cultural diversity. There is need for individuals to be open to challenge and self evaluation in relation to racism and discriminatory practice. There is need for practitioners to examine the value base from which they operate just as has become recognised in child protection work. There is need for understanding and awareness that Black defendants, like any others, are unique identities and cannot be compartmentalised into pre-determined caricatures. This study revealed that many causes of offending which were identified in reports were based upon, or lent themselves to, stereotypical judgements.

Just as in child protection the monocultural perspective of 'orange book' investigations (HMSO, 1988) has been given a multicultural, anti-discriminatory dimension through practice guidelines (see, for example, Race Equality Unit, 1991 and 1995) so there is need for PSR assessments to

148

adopt similar principles to avoid sweeping generalisations about individual people on the basis of perceptions of ethnicity and family origins. As Aktar and Ghataora (1995) note:

> Numerous assumptions and stereotypes exist about Asian communities originating from the Indian sub-continent, even though:
>
> 1. There are predominantly three major religions
>
> 2. There are at least five different languages (and many dialects)
>
> 3. There are different castes and groupings
>
> 4. The identification with 'home' is different e.g. Punjab, Bangladesh, Gujerat, Pakistan, etc.
>
> 5. There are different generations and therefore different experiences and attitudes
>
> 6. There are differences in education, socio-economic classes and different family values and patterns.

It is the racism inherent in white culture which determines that each white family is unique but each Black family can be compartmentalised based on assumptions and stereotypes about life experiences. Similarly, it is the racism inherent in white culture which is so arrogant as to impose a white definition of Black experience and not hear or give credence to each family's definition of reality. Social workers and departments must scrutinise their practice in relation to PSR assessments to ensure that inequalities are not a structurally inherent component of the process.

The Race Equality Unit (1995) in setting out a code of practice in relation to child protection practice argue that the investigation and assessment of risks or abuse should be undertaken in the language of the child and family. Assessments conducted in preparation of PSRs are equally crucial and demand parity in standards of practice. Much can be lost to the enquiry and the report to be presented before the court if crucial information is missed through miscommunication. At this stage in time social work is a long way from being equipped to conduct enquiries in the language of the child and family but as a matter of priority, if departments are to uphold their equal opportunity policies in practice, the necessary training and resources must be found if Black families are to receive a genuinely equal service.

Language, however, is only the starting point. The nature and range of the assessment inquiry is also crucially important. Again, to quote the Race Equality Unit (1995), 'It is important to remember that each family has a set of rules and norms which are unique to it. **The best way to find out what they are - is to ask!**' In 'All Equal Under The Act?' (REU, 1991) an anti-discriminatory assessment framework is presented by Sheila MacDonald which, although designed for child protection work, is transferable to youth justice practice. The checklist guides the practitioner's enquiries. Beginning by placing the family in context it leads on to elicit the family's perceptions of themselves; their experiences of racism; the development of their strengths and the experience of individual family members. It gives consideration to the effect of the enquiry on the family and of having involvement with a social work agency. Also the assessment checklist acknowledges families as experts of their own circumstances and offers opportunity for the family to offer its assessment of itself and the child's view. Finally, it leads the social worker to examine her/his own objectivity in the assessment process by establishing what is the effect of her/his identity; of her/his own definition of 'family'; of the family lifestyles s/he regards as 'acceptable' and asks what is his/her lack of knowledge? Just as these principles apply in child protection work, so too, they apply as markers for good practice in youth justice social work where the liberty of individuals is at stake and of Black defendants in particular.

There is need, therefore, for social workers to empower Black defendants and their families in defining themselves without assumptions being made or attempts at categorisation according to perceptions of similarity in origins or life experiences. There is need to safeguard against the inclusion of material which lends itself to stereotypical judgement. The responsibility for these safeguards rests both with individual practitioners and social services departments. If disparity of sentencing is to be avoided it is incumbent on the individual practitioner to monitor their own work but it is also the responsibility of social services departments to ensure that only quality reports find their way into court.

One of the central features of system management is 'gate-keeping' but unless there is widespread commitment to the principles and procedures of 'gate-keeping' mechanisms Black people will continue to be disadvantaged. In particular, those mechanisms that monitor PSRs need to structured in a way to ensure that reports do not by-pass the system and go directly to court. The system also needs active policing. In cases where authors circumvent the system a safety net needs to be in place to retrieve reports and enforce compliance with the policy and procedures. PSR monitoring should not only ensure that custodial proposals are not made but should also safeguard the practice of presenting an alternative to custody package in each case where a custodial sentence has been indicated.

Effective 'gate-keeping' is not only concerned with individual reports but must also concern itself with trends and patterns. This requires monitoring court outcomes as a whole and in being able to analyse and interpret discernible trends. It is then possible to make changes in policy and practice to address discriminatory trends. Thus, for example, an awareness of the sentencing spiral which has been identified, in which the perception of a greater risk of custody is met with an increased likelihood of community alternative proposals can be detected and addressed.

In addition to practice issues and the operation of system intervention mechanisms there are structural considerations for social services departments to make. Drawing again from developments in the child protection (Northern Curriculum Development Project, 1992) arena chief officers in social services departments should be asking, 'how far do the procedures address the needs of Black children, young people, families and communities? Who sits on the key decision-making bodies, i.e. youth liaison panel/bureau, PSR gate-keeping panel, etc? Are any of these people Black? How have the social services department sought to consult with Black communities about responses to youth crime? Has there been any commitment to, or are there any plans to fund Black projects in the youth justice field?

Organisational changes may also be necessary to address the issues of equality and anti-discriminatory PSR practice. At the time of the study many social services departments were in a stage of transition from genericism to specialised teams. The study showed that most court reports were prepared by workers within generic teams and the frequency of report writing varied from one to six reports in a calendar year. I would argue that the production of so few reports is not conducive to the development of good practice. In these circumstances it might be more appropriate to concentrate PSR preparation within one specialised youth justice team. I believe this view is reinforced through widespread movement towards specialisms and through the detailed knowledge and requirements of 'national standards'.

Finally, it is apparent that issues of 'race' and sentencing are dynamic and operate in a constantly changing environment. This study has provided a snapshot, perhaps with a limited view, of the operation of the youth justice system in one area at a particular moment in time. It is to be hoped that lessons may be learned, locally and beyond, as a result of it. But it is not a once and for all process. It is not a matter of ticking off this item on the agenda and moving onto the next but of constantly re-visiting the sentencing process in relation to 'race' to examine changes in practice. This study has modelled a particular methodology which, I believe, is new to the youth justice arena. It is not a definitive model but one which, no doubt, can be developed and refined through use and re-use elsewhere. I believe that as a result of this study some insights have been gained about the unintended consequences associated with court report practices. I hope as a result that debate will be stimulated around how practice may be further improved which goes beyond the conclusions and recommendations that I have identified. Ultimately, the search is on for practices which will result in equality of sentencing outcome for all defendants irrespective of ethnicity and that there will genuinely be justice for all. That is the challenge that is ahead. Hopefully, this study has contributed by taking a step along the road. The remainder is about practitioners being open to the challenge and prepared to examine and modify practice.

APPENDIX 1

CASE INFORMATION FORM

CASE NO...................

Case Information

D.O.B........................   Area..........................

Last Name...................................   Gender..............................

First Name..................................   Race................................

Proceeding Information

1st Court Appearance.......................   Legal Rep............................

Hearing Date.....................................   SIR Author......................

Court...   Agency........................

Reason for adj. 1.............................   Area..........................

            2.............................   Rec...........................

            3.............................   Other Report: Author...

            4.............................   Rec.............

            5.............................   Remand Type................

            6.............................   Placement....................

No. of adjs...............   Employment/School...............

          Tics............

          Reason for Custody...........

Antecedence

Date	Offence	Outcome

Charge information

Outcome	Amount	Fin.Pen.	Joint/Sole	Endorsemt	Length	Compensn

APPENDIX 2

SOCIAL INQUIRY REPORT CONTENT ANALYSIS EXERCISE

unfavourable I - + - + - + - I favourable

1.	amoral	I - + - + - + - I
2.	epileptic	I - + - + - + - I
3.	impeccable timekeeper	I - + - + - + - I
4.	lacking confidence	I - + - + - + - I
5.	patient	I - + - + - + - I
6.	thoughtful	I - + - + - + - I
7.	aggressive	I - + - + - + - I
8.	emotionally disturbed	I - + - + - + - I
9.	isolated	I - + - + - + - I
10.	lacking commitment	I - + - + - + - I
11.	pleasant	I - + - + - + - I
12.	tense	I - + - + - + - I
13.	angry	I - + - + - + - I
14.	lacking motivation	I - + - + - + - I
15.	pale	I - + - + - + - I
16.	emotionally barren	I - + - + - + - I
17.	immature	I - + - + - + - I
18.	lacking self esteem	I - + - + - + - I
19.	low self worth	I - + - + - + - I
20.	popular	I - + - + - + - I
21.	timid	I - + - + - + - I
22.	agreeable	I - + - + - + - I
23.	easily led	I - + - + - + - I
24.	large	I - + - + - + - I
25.	popular with peers	I - + - + - + - I
26.	placid	I - + - + - + - I
27.	thoughtless	I - + - + - + - I
28.	anxious	I - + - + - + - I

Q

SOCIAL INQUIRY REPORT CONTENT ANALYSIS EXERCISE

unfavourable I - + - + - + - I favourable

1. easily influenced..I - + - + - + - I
2. intelligent...I - + - + - + - I
3. likeable..I - + - + - + - I
4. personable...I - + - + - + - I
5. talkative..I - + - + - + - I
6. anxious about court...I - + - + - + - I
7. apprehensive...I - + - + - + - I
8. enjoys school...I - + - + - + - I
9. indifferent to offending.......................................I - + - + - + - I
10. little insight...I - + - + - + - I
11. apprehensive about court.....................................I - + - + - + - I
12. enjoys a good laugh..I - + - + - + - I
13. indifferent...I - + - + - + - I
14. loves driving..I - + - + - + - I
15. positive attitude...I - + - + - + - I
16. tidy..I - + - + - + - I
17. accepting of responsibility....................................I - + - + - + - I
18. enthusiastic about his Community Service Order.........I - + - + - + - I
19. lively personality...I - + - + - + - I
20. has potential..I - + - + - + - I
21. troubled..I - + - + - + - I
22. accepting of discipline...I - + - + - + - I
23. enthusiastic..I - + - + - + - I
24. interacts well...I - + - + - + - I
25. lazy..I - + - + - + - I
26. polite..I - + - + - + - I
27. tall...I - + - + - + - I
28. has an adult view of himself..................................I - + - + - + - I

W

SOCIAL INQUIRY REPORT CONTENT ANALYSIS EXERCISE

unfavourable I - + - + - + - I favourable

1. extremely unhappy... I - + - + - + - I
2. poor self image... I - + - + - + - I
3. tough... I - + - + - + - I
4. anti-social... I - + - + - + - I
5. frank.. I - + - + - + - I
6. insecure... I - + - + - + - I
7. less mature.. I - + - + - + - I
8. poor dexterity.. I - + - + - + - I
9. thin.. I - + - + - + - I
10. is accepted... I - + - + - + - I
11. failed to co-operate.. I - + - + - + - I
12. interested in sport.. I - + - + - + - I
13. loyal to his family.. I - + - + - + - I
14. participates well... I - + - + - + - I
15. poor co-ordination.. I - + - + - + - I
16. tough exterior.. I - + - + - + - I
17. aware... I - + - + - + - I
18. friendly.. I - + - + - + - I
19. interested in art.. I - + - + - + - I
20. mature.. I - + - + - + - I
21. punctual... I - + - + - + - I
22. unloved.. I - + - + - + - I
23. below average weight.. I - + - + - + - I
24. fretful... I - + - + - + - I
25. unwilling.. I - + - + - + - I
26. passive... I - + - + - + - I
27. mixed race.. I - + - + - + - I
28. introverted.. I - + - + - + - I

E

SOCIAL INQUIRY REPORT CONTENT ANALYSIS EXERCISE

unfavourable I - + - + - + - I favourable

1. of few words..I - + - + - + - I
2. below average ability..I - + - + - + - I
3. full of bravado...I - + - + - + - I
4. full of energy..I - + - + - + - I
5. a rebel..I - + - + - + - I
6. bitter...I - + - + - + - I
7. fearful..I - + - + - + - I
8. initiating no conversation...................................I - + - + - + - I
9. morose...I - + - + - + - I
10. quiet..I - + - + - + - I
11. upset..I - + - + - + - I
12. a bully..I - + - + - + - I
13. forthcoming..I - + - + - + - I
14. a quick sense of humour......................................I - + - + - + - I
15. bright...I - + - + - + - I
16. attached to his mother.......................................I - + - + - + - I
17. insolent...I - + - + - + - I
18. monosyllabic...I - + - + - + - I
19. quietly spoken...I - + - + - + - I
20. underweight..I - + - + - + - I
21. blasé..I - + - + - + - I
22. sometimes bad tempered.......................................I - + - + - + - I
23. an impressionable girl.......................................I - + - + - + - I
24. responsive...I - + - + - + - I
25. unhappy with peers...I - + - + - + - I
26. bouts of aggression..I - + - + - + - I
27. has ability..I - + - + - + - I
28. independent..I - + - + - + - I

R

SOCIAL INQUIRY REPORT CONTENT ANALYSIS EXERCISE

unfavourable I - + - + - + - I favourable

1.	mild mannered..	I - + - + - + - I
2.	regular school attendance..............................	I - + - + - + - I
3.	uncaring...	I - + - + - + - I
4.	has better communication skills.....................	I - + - + - + - I
5.	influence others...	I - + - + - + - I
6.	regrets his actions...	I - + - + - + - I
7.	unco-operative manner..................................	I - + - + - + - I
8.	bored..	I - + - + - + - I
9.	athletic...	I - + - + - + - I
10.	in need of direction.......................................	I - + - + - + - I
11.	opts out..	I - + - + - + - I
12.	regrets offending..	I - + - + - + - I
13.	uncommunicative...	I - + - + - + - I
14.	behaves well at home....................................	I - + - + - + - I
15.	ashamed...	I - + - + - + - I
16.	impulsive..	I - + - + - + - I
17.	reticent...	I - + - + - + - I
18.	unwilling to conform.....................................	I - + - + - + - I
19.	chirpy...	I - + - + - + - I
20.	active..	I - + - + - + - I
21.	keen to find employment...............................	I - + - + - + - I
22.	perpetrator...	I - + - + - + - I
23.	remorseful..	I - + - + - + - I
24.	unwilling to conform to school routine.........	I - + - + - + - I
25.	charming..	I - + - + - + - I
26.	awkward...	I - + - + - + - I
27.	reserved...	I - + - + - + - I
28.	is a changed person.......................................	I - + - + - + - I

T

SOCIAL INQUIRY REPORT CONTENT ANALYSIS EXERCISE

unfavourable I - + - + - + - I favourable

1. amiable..I - + - + - + - I
2. keeps himself clean..................................... I - + - + - + - I
3. is picked on..I - + - + - + - I
4. rejected..I - + - + - + - I
5. unsettled at school...................................... I - + - + - + - I
6. caring.. I - + - + - + - I
7. has affection for his family...........................I - + - + - + - I
8. is easily bored...I - + - + - + - I
9. slightly tragic...I - + - + - + - I
10. respectful.. I - + - + - + - I
11. unresponsive.. I - + - + - + - I
12. confused..I - + - + - + - I
13. amenable...I - + - + - + - I
14. keen...I - + - + - + - I
15. scapegoat.. I - + - + - + - I
16. responsible..I - + - + - + - I
17. a victim of circumstance..............................I - + - + - + - I
18. clean..I - + - + - + - I
19. cares..I - + - + - + - I
20. relaxed demeanour.....................................I - + - + - + - I
21. capable...I - + - + - + - I
22. amicable...I - + - + - + - I
23. abusive...I - + - + - + - I
24. a show off... I - + - + - + - I
25. self absorbed..I - + - + - + - I
26. vulnerable... I - + - + - + - I
27. careful.. I - + - + - + - I
28. an attractive girl..I - + - + - + - I

Y

SOCIAL INQUIRY REPORT CONTENT ANALYSIS EXERCISE

unfavourable I - + - + - + - I favourable

1.	sensible	I - + - + - + - I
2.	settled at school	I - + - + - + - I
3.	callous	I - + - + - + - I
4.	arrogant	I - + - + - + - I
5.	laughs appropriately	I - + - + - + - I
6.	nervous	I - + - + - + - I
7.	settled	I - + - + - + - I
8.	verbally abusive	I - + - + - + - I
9.	cheerful	I - + - + - + - I
10.	periods of good behaviour	I - + - + - + - I
11.	shows acts of kindness	I - + - + - + - I
12.	a comic	I - + - + - + - I
13.	good behaviour at home	I - + - + - + - I
14.	of average intelligence	I - + - + - + - I
15.	has no empathy	I - + - + - + - I
16.	self motivated	I - + - + - + - I
17.	volatile	I - + - + - + - I
18.	complex	I - + - + - + - I
19.	uncontrollable	I - + - + - + - I
20.	concerned	I - + - + - + - I
21.	has a good sense of humour	I - + - + - + - I
22.	physically presentable	I - + - + - + - I
23.	has no ambition	I - + - + - + - I
24.	has a sense of maturity	I - + - + - + - I
25.	unruly	I - + - + - + - I
26.	commitment is short-lived	I - + - + - + - I
27.	rude	I - + - + - + - I
28.	a steady worker	I - + - + - + - I

U

SOCIAL INQUIRY REPORT CONTENT ANALYSIS EXERCISE

unfavourable I - + - + - + - I favourable

1. co-operative... I - + - + - + - I
2. has good dress sense................................ I - + - + - + - I
3. smiles a lot.. I - + - + - + - I
4. naive... I - + - + - + - I
5. sensitive.. I - + - + - + - I
6. violent... I - + - + - + - I
7. communicates quite easily......................... I - + - + - + - I
8. genuinely sorry... I - + - + - + - I
9. laughs a lot.. I - + - + - + - I
10. nicer.. I - + - + - + - I
11. sensitive about his size.............................. I - + - + - + - I
12. withdrawn.. I - + - + - + - I
13. short-sighted as to consequences................ I - + - + - + - I
14. communicates easily................................. I - + - + - + - I
15. devious.. I - + - + - + - I
16. unable to discuss feelings.......................... I - + - + - + - I
17. has a strong personality............................ I - + - + - + - I
18. considerate.. I - + - + - + - I
19. deviant... I - + - + - + - I
20. no sign of regret....................................... I - + - + - + - I
21. smart... I - + - + - + - I
22. willing... I - + - + - + - I
23. conducts himself well................................ I - + - + - + - I
24. low tolerance level to stress....................... I - + - + - + - I
25. selfish.. I - + - + - + - I
26. courteous... I - + - + - + - I
27. high spirits... I - + - + - + - I
28. short sighted.. I - + - + - + - I

I

SOCIAL INQUIRY REPORT CONTENT ANALYSIS EXERCISE

unfavourable I - + - + - + - I favourable

1. low tolerance threshold.................................... I - + - + - + - I
2. a natural wit.. I - + - + - + - I
3. streetwise.. I - + - + - + - I
4. well liked... I - + - + - + - I
5. communicative.. I - + - + - + - I
6. like a wild animal... I - + - + - + - I
7. shy... I - + - + - + - I
8. well mannered.. I - + - + - + - I
9. confident.. I - + - + - + - I
10. healthy... I - + - + - + - I
11. not very forthcoming.. I - + - + - + - I
12. strong... I - + - + - + - I
13. well built.. I - + - + - + - I
14. conscientious.. I - + - + - + - I
15. happy... I - + - + - + - I
16. likes to work hard.. I - + - + - + - I
17. shows no remorse.. I - + - + - + - I
18. strong willed... I - + - + - + - I
19. self confident.. I - + - + - + - I
20. well cared for.. I - + - + - + - I
21. distant.. I - + - + - + - I
22. slightly built... I - + - + - + - I
23. defiant.. I - + - + - + - I
24. had a happy childhood...................................... I - + - + - + - I
25. lonely... I - + - + - + - I
26. not usually aggressive...................................... I - + - + - + - I
27. slim.. I - + - + - + - I
28. well behaved... I - + - + - + - I

O

SOCIAL INQUIRY REPORT CONTENT ANALYSIS EXERCISE

unfavourable I - + - + - + - I favourable

1. small in stature...I - + - + - + - I
2. worried about custody.....................................I - + - + - + - I
3. depressed..I - + - + - + - I
4. honest...I - + - + - + - I
5. a little boy...I - + - + - + - I
6. not without ability..I - + - + - + - I
7. short...I - + - + - + - I
8. worried...I - + - + - + - I
9. damaged..I - + - + - + - I
10. helpful around the house.................................I - + - + - + - I
11. stockily built...I - + - + - + - I
12. deprived...I - + - + - + - I
13. helpful..I - + - + - + - I
14. has little pleasure in life..................................I - + - + - + - I
15. not academically inclined................................I - + - + - + - I
16. signs of disturbance..I - + - + - + - I
17. will work hard..I - + - + - + - I
18. sad...I - + - + - + - I
19. disturbed...I - + - + - + - I
20. helps mother..I - + - + - + - I
21. lively..I - + - + - + - I
22. has an obsession with fire.................................I - + - + - + - I
23. sorry...I - + - + - + - I
24. works hard...I - + - + - + - I
25. does not smile..I - + - + - + - I
26. difficult...I - + - + - + - I
27. humorous...I - + - + - + - I
28. has little ambition...I - + - + - + - I

P

SOCIAL INQUIRY REPORT CONTENT ANALYSIS EXERCISE

unfavourable I - + - + - + - I favourable

1.   open..I - + - + - + - I
2.   surly... I - + - + - + - I
3.   would not help himself..................................I - + - + - + - I
4.   difficult to talk to..I - + - + - + - I
5.   very good...I - + - + - + - I
6.   does what he is told...................................... I - + - + - + - I
7.   holds considerable affection for his mother..................I - + - + - + - I
8.   little motivation.. I - + - + - + - I
9.   optimistic...I - + - + - + - I
10. sickly...I - + - + - + - I
11. warm... I - + - + - + - I
12. has limited horizons......................................I - + - + - + - I
13. determined...I - + - + - + - I
14. outgoing..I - + - + - + - I
15. suffers from asthma......................................I - + - + - + - I
16. a willing party in the offences......................I - + - + - + - I
17. is limited...I - + - + - + - I
18. displays talent..I - + - + - + - I
19. hard to settle.. I - + - + - + - I
20. low level of retention..................................I - + - + - + - I
21. overawed..I - + - + - + - I
22. has a short concentration span.......................I - + - + - + - I
23. wilful..I - + - + - + - I
24. disruptive..I - + - + - + - I
25. young.. I - + - + - + - I
26. has a limited appreciation of his problems................... I - + - + - + - I
27. overweight...I - + - + - + - I
28. sociable..I - + - + - + - I

A

SOCIAL INQUIRY REPORT CONTENT ANALYSIS EXERCISE

unfavourable I - + - + - + - I favourable

1. worldly wise.. I - + - + - + - I
2. prone to temper tantrums...I - + - + - + - I
3. able to make steady progress when motivated..............I - + - + - + - I
4. anxious to gain approval.. I - + - + - + - I
5. examining his identity.. I - + - + - + - I
6. a degree of deviousness...I - + - + - + - I
7. unable to control his temper..I - + - + - + - I
8. finds it difficult to articulate thoughts and feelings.......I - + - + - + - I
9. problems controlling his temper..................................I - + - + - + - I
10. refuses to accept responsibility..................................... I - + - + - + - I
11. able to lead and provoke trouble.................................. I - + - + - + - I
12. a willingness to participate in group activities.............. I - + - + - + - I
13. influenced by local groups.. I - + - + - + - I
14. relates the stupidity of the offence............................... I - + - + - + - I
15. gets on well with siblings... I - + - + - + - I
16. almost total lack of co-operation...................................I - + - + - + - I
17. does not find it easy to make friends............................I - + - + - + - I
18. gets bored quickly... I - + - + - + - I
19. wishes to present as physically strong..........................I - + - + - + - I
20. able to handle himself...I - + - + - + - I
21. gives the impression of being clever.............................I - + - + - + - I
22. capable of solving his own problems.............................I - + - + - + - I
23. difficulty in resisting pressure from older boys.............I - + - + - + - I
24. rarely shows his good side.. I - + - + - + - I
25. does not know the difference between right and wrong I - + - + - + - I

S

Bibliography

Adams, R., Allard, S., Baldwin, J. and Thomas, J. (1981), *A Measure of Diversion? Case studies in Intermediate Treatment,* National Youth Bureau, Leicester.

Atkar, S., Ghataora, R. K. and Klair, S. K.(1995), *Asian Children and Families Project: Interim Report,* NSPCC/University of Warwick, Coventry.

Baldwin, N., Johansen, P. and Seale, A. (1989/90), *Race in Child Protection: A code of practice,* Black and White Alliance, Race Equality Unit (NISW), Huddersfield.

Ball, C. (1984), 'Reports for the Juvenile Court', *Justice and the Law,* Assn. for Juvenile Justice, pp. 9-18.

Ball, W. and Solomos, J. (1990), *Race and Local Politics,* Macmillan.

Banton, M. and Harwood, J. (1975), *The Race Concept,* David and Charles.

Bean, P. (1971), 'Social Inquiry Reports and the Decision Making Process', *Family Law,* Vol. 1, No. 6. pp. 174 - 178.

Bean, P. (1976), *Rehabilitation and Deviance,* Routledge and Kegan Paul, London.

Bell, A. and Gibson, P. (1991), 'Tackling the Dilemmas for Policy and Practice in Justice Systems Divided by Age', *Juvenile Justice in the New Europe,* Social Service Monographs: Research in Practice, Sheffield.

Benyon, J. (1986), *A Tail of Failure: Race and Policing,* Centre for Research in Ethnic Relations.

Berry, S. (1984), *Ethnic Minorities and the Juvenile Court,* Nottinghamshire Social Services Department, Nottingham.

Blumer, H. (1956), 'Sociological analysis and the variable', *American Sociological Research,* Vol. 21, pp. 633-60.

Bottoms, A. (1974), ' On the decriminalisation of the English Juvenile Courts', *Crime, Criminology and Public Policy*, Heinneman, London.

Bottoms, A. and Stelman, A. (1988), *Social Inquiry Reports*, Wildwood House, Aldershot.

Branch, G. (1991), *'Longer Sentences for Blacks blamed on Probation Officers'*, Unpublished Paper, University of Warwick, Coventry.

Brophy, J. and Smart, P. (eds.), (1985), *Women in Law*, Routledge and Kegan Paul, London.

Brown, S. (1990), *Social Information and its 'usefulness' in the Juvenile Court: An analysis of Magistrates' Accounts in Organisational Context*, PhD Thesis, Teesside Polytechnic Department of Administrative and Social Studies.

Brown, S. (1991), *Magistrates at Work*, Open University Press.

Chiquada, R. (1988), 'The Criminalisation and Imprisonment of Black Women', *Probation Journal*, Sept. 1989.

Christie, N. (1974), 'Utility and Social Values', *Crime and Criminology*, Heinneman, London.

Cicourel, A. (1964), *Method and Measurement in Sociology*, New York Free Press, New York.

Cohen, S. (1985), *Visions of Social Control: Crime, Punishment and Classification*, Polity Press, Cambridge.

Concise Oxford Dictionary, (1990), Clarendon Press, Oxford.

Crow, I. and Cove, J. (1984), 'Ethnic Minorities in the Courts', *Criminal Law Review*, July 1984, pp 413-417.

Crowther, E. (1991), Comments made in *Public Eye*, television broadcast, 1 March, 1991, BBC News and Current Affairs, London.

Davies, B. (1980), *'Intermediate Treatment as Social Policy - A Critical History'*, Unpublished Paper, University of Warwick, Coventry.

de Gale, H., Hanlon, P., Hubbard, M. and Morgan, S. (1993), *Improving Practice in the Criminal justice System*, Northern Curriculum Development Project, CCETSW, Leeds.

De la Motta, C. (1984), *'Blacks in the Criminal Justice System'*, Unpublished Msc. dissertation, Aston University, Birmingham.

De May, H. (1971) 'Delinquency Control and the Treatment Model', *British Journal of Criminology*.

Denman, G. (1982), *Intensive Intermediate Treatment with Juvenile Offenders: A Handbook of Assessment and Groupwork Practice*, Centre of Youth Crime and Community, Lancaster.

Dominelli, L. (1988), *Anti-racist Social Work*, Macmillan, London.

Dominelli, L. (1990), 'An Uncaring Profession? An examination of Racism in Social Work', *Racism in Social Work,* Macmillan, London.

Edwards, S. (1984), *Women on Trial,* Manchester University Press, Manchester.

Ely, P. and Denney, D. (1987), *Social Work in a Multi-racial Society,* Gower, Aldershot.

Emmins, C. (1985), *A Practical Approach to Sentencing,* Financial Training Publications.

Evans, R. (1982), *The Theoretical Foundations of Doing IT,* Social Work Monograph No. 12, University of East Anglia, Norwich.

Fitzgerald, M. (1991), *Ethnic Minorities and the Criminal Justice System: Research Issues,* Unpublished Paper presented to British Criminology Conference, 1991.

Fludger, N. (1981), *Ethnic Minorities in Borstal,* Home Office, London.

Foster, J. (1989), *Villains: Crime and Community in the Inner City,* Routledge, London.

Giller, H. (n.d.), *Monitoring, Evaluating and Changing Local Criminal Justice Systems,* Social Information Systems, Lancaster.

Gilroy, P. (1990), 'The End of Anti-racism', *Race and Local Politics,* Macmillan.

Glasgow, D. (1980), *The Black Underclass,* Jossey Bass, New York.

Gordon, P. (1983), *White Law: Racism in the Police, Courts and Prisons,* Pluto, London.

Gordon, P. (1990) 'The New Right and Anti-racism', *Race and Local Politics,* Macmillan.

Greater London Council, (1984), *Policing London,* GLC Police Committee Support Unit, London.

Griffith, J. (1977), *The Politics of the Judiciary,* Fontana.

Guest, M. (1984), *A comparative Analysis of the Career Patterns of Black and White Offenders,* Unpublished Msc. thesis, Cranfield Institute, Bedfordshire.

Hall, P., Land, H., Parker, R. and Webb, A. (1978), *Change, Choice and Conflict in Social Policy,* Heinneman, London.

Hall, S. (1980), *Drifting into a Law and Order Society,* Cobden Trust.

Harris, R. and Webb, D. (1987), *Welfare Power and Justice,* Tavistock, London.

Hazell, A. (1987), *Social Inquiry Reports: A Guide to Good Practice,* Unpublished Paper presented to BASW Study Day 21.

Heidensohn, F. (1987), 'Women and Crime: Questions for Criminology', *Gender, Crime and Justice,* Open University.

Hill, G. (1985), 'The Impact of the 1982 C.J.A. on Juveniles', *Training Anthology,* Yorkshire and Humberside IT Assn., Leeds.

HMSO, (1927), *Report of the Committee on Children and Young Persons,* (Moloney Report), HMSO, London.

HMSO, (1960), *Report of the Committee on Children and Young Persons,* (Ingleby Report), Cmnd. 1191, HMSO, London.

HMSO, (1961), *Report of the Interdepartmental Committee on the Business of the Criminal Courts,* (Streatfield Report), Cmnd. 1289, HMSO, London.

HMSO, (1962), *Report of the Departmental Committee on the Probation Service,* (Morrison Report), HMSO, London.

HMSO, (1964), *Children and Young Persons: Scotland,* (Kilbrandon Report), Cmnd. 2306, HMSO, Edinburgh.

HMSO, (1965), *'The Child, The Family and The Young Offender',* Government White Paper, Cmnd. 2742, HMSO, London.

HMSO, (1968), *'Children in Trouble',* Government White Paper, Cmnd. 3601, HMSO, London.

HMSO, (1981), *The Sentence of the Court,* HMSO, London.

Home Office, (1971a), *Circular 28/1971,* Home Office.

Home Office, (1971b), *Circular 59/1971,* Home Office.

Home Office, (1974), *Circular 194/1974,* Home Office.

Home Office, (1979), *Criminal Statistics,* Home Office.

Home Office, (1981), *Criminal Statistics,* Home Office.

Home Office, (1983a), *Circular 17/1983, Social Inquiry Reports: General Guidance on Contents,* Home Office.

Home Office, (1983b), *Circular 18/1983, Social Inquiry Reports: Recommendations Relevant to Sentencing,* Home Office.

Home Office, (1986a), *Criminal Statistics,* Home Office.

Home Office, (1986b), *Circular 92/1986, Social Inquiry Reports.* Home Office.

Home Office, (1988), *Criminal Statistics,* Home Office.

Home Office, (1990), *A Digest of information on the Criminal Justice System: Crime and Justice in England and Wales,* Home Office Research and Statistics Unit.

Hood, R. (1992), *Race and Sentencing: A study in the Crown Court,* Commission for Racial Equality, Clarendon Press, Oxford.

Hudson, B. (1989), *Discrimination and Disparity: Researching the Influence of Race on Sentencing,* Unpublished Paper presented to British Criminology Conference, 1989.

170

Husband, C. (1986), 'Racism, Prejudice and Social Policy', *Race and Social Work: A Guide to Training*, Tavistock, London.

Keith, M, and Murji, K. (1990), 'Reifying Crime, Legitimising Racism: Policing, Local Authorities and Left Realism', *Race and Local Politics*, Macmillan.

Kinsey, R., Lea, J. and Young, J. (1986), *Losing the Fight against Crime*, Blackwell, Oxford.

Kirk, B. (1988), *The Development of the Juvenile Justice System*, Unpublished Paper, Coventry (Lanchester) Polytechnic.

Kirk, B. (1994), *An Examination of 'Race' and the Juvenile Justice System: A Case Study in Wolverhampton in 1990*, MA Thesis, University of Warwick.

Landau, S. and Nathan, G. (1983), 'Selecting delinquents for cautioning in the London Metropolitan area', *British Journal of Criminology*, Vol. 23, No. 2. pp. 128-149.

Lea, J. and Young, J. (1982), 'Riots in Britain', *Policing the Riots*, Junction Books.

Lea, J. and Young, J. (1984), *What is to be done about Law and Order?* Penguin.

Legal Action Group, (1982), 'Race and Sentencing', *LAG Bulletin*.

Longford, Lord, (1964), *Crime - A Challenge to us all* (Longford Report), Labour Party, London.

Lorde, A. (1984), *Sister Outsider: Essays and Speeches by Audre Lorde*, Crossing Press, New York.

Mahoney, D. (1991), *Sentencing in the Youth Court*, Unpublished Paper presented at British Criminology Conference, July 1991.

Mair, G. (1985), 'Working Together? The System in Action', *Managing Criminal Justice: A Collection of Papers*, Home Office Research and Planning Unit, London.

Mair, G. (1986), 'Ethnic Minorities, Probation and the Magistrates' Court', *British Journal of Criminology*, Vol. 26, April 1986.

Matza, D. (1964), *Delinquency and Drift*, I. Wiley and Son, New York.

McConville, M. and Baldwin, J. (1982), 'The Influence of Race on Sentencing in England', *Criminal Law Review*, pp 652-658, 1986.

McDonald, S. (1991), *All Equal Under the Act? - a practical guide to the Children Act 1989 for social workers*, Race Equality Unit, London.

Moore, T. (1985), 'Whose Justice?', *Justice and the Law*, Assn. for Juvenile Justice.

Morris, A. and Giller, H. (1987), *Understanding Juvenile Justice*, Croom Helm, Beckenham.

Moser, C. and Kalton, G. (1973), *Survey Methods in Social Investigation*, Heinneman, London.

Mould, E. (1978), 'Chivalry and Paternalism: Disparities of Treatment in the Criminal Justice System', *Western Political Quarterly*, Vol. 31, pp. 416-30.

Moxon, D., Jones, P. and Tarling, R. (1985), *Juvenile Sentencing: Is there a tariff?* Home Office Research and Planning Unit, Paper 32, Home Office.

NACRO, (1988), *Race and Justice for Young Offenders,* NACRO, London.

O'Leary, P. (1990), *The use of Social Stereotype of Womanhood in the Criminal Justice System*, Unpublished MA dissertation, University of Warwick.

Ouseley, H. (1990), 'Resisting Institutional Change', *Race and Local Politics*, Macmillan.

Paley, J., Thorpe, D., Smith, D. and Green, C. (1980), *Out of Care: The Community Support of Juvenile Offenders*, George Allen and Unwin.

Parker, H., Sumner, M. and Jarvis, G. (1989), *Unmasking the Magistrates*, Open University Press.

Parsloe, P. (1976), 'Social Work and the Justice Model', *British Journal of Social Work*, Vol. 6, No. 1.

Pearson, G. (1978) , 'Social Work and Law and Order', *Social Work Today*, 4 April 1978.

Pearson, G. (1983), *Hooligans: A History of Respectable Fears*, Macmillan.

Pearson, G. (1985), 'Hooligans in History', *Training Anthology*, Yorkshire and Humberside IT Assn.

Perry, F. (1974), *Information for the Courts: A New Look at Social Inquiry Reports*, University of Cambridge, Institute of Criminology, Cambridge.

Pimm, L. and Lines, P. (1987), *Report on the Birmingham Court Report Monitoring Exercise,* West Midlands Probation Service.

Pinchbeck, I. and Hewitt, M. (1973), *Children in English Society, Vol. 2, From the Eighteenth Century to the Children Act, 1948*, Routledge, London.

Pinder, R. (1984), *Probation Work in a Multi-racial Society; Treating all the same?*, West Yorkshire Probation Service.

Pitts, J. (1988), *The Politics of Crime*, Sage, London.

Policy Studies Institute, (1983), *Police and People in London*, Policy Studies Institute.

Powell, M. (1985), 'Court Work', *Working with Offenders,* Macmillan, London.

Pratt, J. (1989), 'Corporatism: The Third Model of Juvenile Justice', *British Journal of Criminology,* pp 236ff.

Race Equality Unit, (1992), *All Equal Under the Act? - a practical guide to the Children Act 1989 for social workers*, Race Equality Unit, London.

Race Equality Unit, (1989), *Race in Child Protection: A Code of Practice*, Race Equality Unit, London..

Raynor, P. (1985), *Social Work, Justice and Control*, Basil Blackwell, Oxford.

Raynor, P. (1985a), 'Social Inquiries, Diversion and the Juvenile Tariff', *Training Anthology*, Yorkshire and Humberside Intermediate Treatment Association.

Reynolds, F. (1982), 'Social Work Influence in Juvenile Court Disposals', *British Journal of Social Work*, Vol. 12, pp 65-76.

Richman, J. and Draycott, A. (1990), *Stone's Justices' Manual*, Butterworths, London.

Rutherford, A. (1986), *Growing out of Crime*, Penguin, London.

Rutherford, A. (1992), *Growing out of Crime: The New Era*, Waterside, Winchester.

Schur, E. (1973) *Radical Non Intervention*, Prentice-Hall, Englewood Cliffs.

Shallice, A. and Gordon, P. (1990), *Black People, White Justice*, Runnymede Trust, London.

Silverman, D. (1985), *Qualitative Methodology and Sociology*, Gower, Aldershot.

Smith, D. (1985), 'The Origins and Aims of the 1982 Criminal Justice Act', *Training Anthology*, Yorkshire and Humberside Intermediate Treatment Assn.

Smith, D. and Gray, J. (1983) *Police and People in London IV: The Police in Action*, Policy Studies Institute.

Solomos, J. (1992), *Race and Racism in Contemporary Britain*, Macmillan.

Stevens, S. and Willis, C. (1979), *Race, Crime and Arrests*, Research Study 58, Home Office, London.

Taylor, I. Walton, P. and Young, J. (1973), *The New Criminology: For a Social Theory of Deviance*, Routledge and Kegan Paul, London.

Taylor, W. (1981), *Probation and After-care in a Multi-racial Society*, Commission for Racial Equality, London.

Thorpe, J. (1979), *Social Inquiry Reports: A Survey*, Research Study No. 48, Home Office, London.

Tipler, J. (1985), *Juvenile Justice in Hackney*, Social Services Department, London Borough of Hackney.

Tipler, J. (1986), *Is Justice Colour Blind?* Social Services Department, London Borough of Hackney.

Tipler, J. (1989), 'Colour-conscious Justice', *Community Care,* 30 March 1989.

Unnever, J. Frazier, C. and Henrietta, J. (1980), 'Race Differences in Criminal Sentencing', *Sociological Quarterly*, Vol. 21, pp 197-205.

Voakes, R. and Fowler, Q. (1989), *Sentencing, Race and Social Enquiry Reports*, West Yorkshire Probation Service, Bradford.

Walker, H. (1985), 'Women's Issues in Probation Practice', *Working with Offenders*, Macmillan, London.

Walker, M. Jefferson, T. and Seneviratne, M. (1989), *Race and Criminal Justice in a Provincial City*, Paper presented at British Criminology Conference.

Waters, R. (1991), *Ethnic Minorities and the Criminal Justice System*, Avebury, Aldershot.

Whitehouse, P. (1986), 'Race and the Criminal Justice System', *Race and Social Work: A Guide to Training,* Tavistock, London.

Wiggin, P. (1981), *Justice or Treatment: A study of Policy Towards Juvenile Delinquents in England and Wales*, Child Care Study No. 5, Church of England Children's Society, London.

Wolverhampton Borough Council, (1988), *Juveniles Residing in Wolverhampton Appearing Before the Wolverhampton Juvenile Court: 1.1.1988 to 31.12.1988,* Wolverhampton Borough Council.

Wolverhampton Careers Service, (1988), Personal Correspondence.

Wolverhampton Careers Service, (1990), Personal Correspondence.

Worrall, A. (1990), *Offending Women*, Routledge, London.

Young, J. (1991), Comments made on 'Public Eye', television programme broadcast 1 March, 1991, BBC News and Current Affairs.